HEADLEY AND I

S. HUSSAIN ZAIDI is a veteran of investigative, crime and terror reporting. He has worked for *The Asian Age, Mumbai Mirror, Mid-Day* and *The Indian Express*. His previous books include bestsellers like *Black Friday, Mafia Queens of Mumbai* and the more recent *Dongri to Dubai: Six Decades of the Mumbai Mafia*. Zaidi is also associate producer for the HBO movie, *Terror in Mumbai*, based on the 26/11 terror strikes. He lives with his family in Mumbai.

PRAISE FOR S. HUSSAIN ZAIDI

'No reporter covering this beat has been more assiduous or influential than S. Hussain Zaidi, whose work has appeared in several newspapers over the past 15 years, including *The Indian Express*, *Mid-Day* and *The Asian Age*' —Che Kurrien in GQ

'His writerly voice has always been that of a newspaperman: controlled, grim . . . His writing rarely veers from straightforward agglomeration of facts, but he displays an acute eye for emotional detail' —*Mint*

'The undeniable strength of *Black Friday* is the depth and intelligence with which Zaidi portrays the bombers themselves. In penetrating this closed world, Zaidi ridicules the shorthand caricature of terrorists so popular nowadays: that they are "evil", "fanatic" or "mad". Instead, we get to read about ordinary men who start out with earthly motivations and none-too-resolute convictions but who ultimately come to embrace terror. Such portraits reveal more about the roots of terrorism than a thousand theories about the clash of civilizations could.' —*Time Magazine*

'*Dongri to Dubai* is an intermittently fascinating account of Dawood Ibrahim's transformation from neighbourhood thug to global gangster. S. Hussain Zaidi has built up a reputation for scoops' —Nandini Ramnath, *Timeout*

'The stories of the 13 women [in *Mafia Queens of Mumbai*] vibrate with drama, intrigue and unexpected pathos' —Zara Murao in *Hindustan Times*

'*Mafia Queens of Mumbai* . . . is a page-turner with saucy excerpts from the lives of smugglers' molls and underworld doyennes' —Vishwas Kulkarni, *Mumbai Mirror*

'Despite it being a work of non-fiction, *Dongri to Dubai* can read something like a script of an exciting movie. There is great detailing even with minor characters' —*Sunday Guardian*

'The strength of *Dongri to Dubai* lies in the simplicity of the narrative and language. It is an eye opener to various events that shaped Mumbai and India' —*Open*

'*Dongri to Dubai* . . . is a thrill-a-minute page-turner' —*Sunday Mid-day*

'[*Dongri to Dubai*] is a compelling portrait of the dons and the hit men' —Naresh Fernandes in *The Hindu*

HEADLEY AND I

S. Hussain Zaidi

with

Rahul Bhatt

Foreword by Mahesh Bhatt

HarperCollins *Publishers* India
a joint venture with

New Delhi

First published in India in 2012 by
HarperCollins *Publishers* India
a joint venture with
The India Today Group

ISBN: 978-93-5029-572-4

2 4 6 8 10 9 7 5 3 1

HarperCollins *Publishers*
A-53, Sector 57, Noida, Uttar Pradesh 201301, India
77-85 Fulham Palace Road, London W6 8JB, United Kingdom
Hazelton Lanes, 55 Avenue Road, Suite 2900, Toronto, Ontario M5R 3L2
and 1995 Markham Road, Scarborough, Ontario M1B 5M8, Canada
25 Ryde Road, Pymble, Sydney, NSW 2073, Australia
31 View Road, Glenfield, Auckland 10, New Zealand
10 East 53rd Street, New York NY 10022, USA

Typeset in 13/16 Calibri MT, Rockwell Regular and Linden Hill Regular at
SÜRYA

Printed and bound at
Manipal Technologies Ltd., Manipal

FOREWORD

'You have a choice, son. Either you go through life whining like a victim, wearing your troubled childhood like a badge on your sleeve and earning sympathy from people who don't matter or care, or you become a survivor. You use your pain and your rage as fuel to hurl you to the top of the heap. I did the latter. That is why I am where I am. Do you know, all said and done, you and I do have one thing in common. A childhood without a father . . .'

I was talking to Rahul as we travelled through the vast, awe-inspiring landscape of Spiti. This was literally God's land. Thanks to my daughter Pooja, who was shooting her first directorial venture there, we were in Kibber, the highest motorable village in the world. This had become a rare opportunity for Rahul and me to be alone together after many years. In fact, after that painful night in 1985, when I had walked away from his home, when he was barely three years old. Little did I know that, years later, life would deal him a hand whereby he would be forced to make that choice.

'Why do you want to call him Mohammed, beta?' asked my mother, who had spent most of her life concealing her Muslim identity. She feared that what we called a secular India still viewed Muslims as 'the other'.

'Because I want your Islamic legacy to continue through my son in some small way,' I replied.

My mother finally prevailed by ganging up with my Anglo-Indian Christian wife and my very reasonable, sage-like Maharashtrian Brahmin neighbour, and my son was called Rahul, alias Sunny.

In retrospect, I shudder to think what would have happened to my son in 2009, if he had been called Mohammed Bhatt.

Rahul was born to help stitch together my relationship with my childhood sweetheart, Lorraine Bright (Kiran Bhatt), which was by then in tatters. And I remember embracing the role of fatherhood once again with all my heart and soul.

A rare, early memory of Sunny and me together surfaces. Dawn is breaking over Pali Hill. I am an unemployed, struggling film-maker. I am wheeling Sunny in his pram on the deserted slopes of an affluent Pali Hill, taking him for a morning walk. A very happily drunk actor of some repute, returning from a late-night party, appears on the scene. Seeing me in an unlikely parental avatar with my little boy melts his heart. Bending down to Sunny, and breathing alcoholic fumes all over him, he gushes, 'Will you remember how your father is taking you for this morning walk when everyone is sleeping? Or will you, too, like all sons, forget?' Saying this, he slobbers a kiss on me and sways off to his car. Don't ask me why, but that very funny memory moves me today.

Memories . . . Memories are the stuff of life. Man is memory after all. When I look within, I find that I don't have memories of me with my son. A flourishing career, a second marriage, my quest for truth, all perhaps contributed in a way to clutter my life up, and leave me less and less time to spend with my son. (I hardly spent any time with my two daughters from my second marriage either during this phase.) Though I always continued to be a provider in every way, and a parental figure who stood by him through thick and thin, I guess the small things were overlooked. I was not able to give him the time of day when it came to the everyday things, the mundane, the 'normal' time that father and son get to spend with each other. Like the time I spent with him when I was a failure and unemployed. The bitter truth was that I had become what I hated. All my life I blamed my own father for not doing these things with me. And now I was doing the same. All I wanted was to be able to correct this. But I didn't know how.

And then one day fate intervened to give me what I wanted. In fact, it seemed like the entire universe, no less, had conspired to give me a very bizarre chance to realize this desire!

'I think this David Headley that the intelligence agencies are talking about is the guy I got to know through my fitness buddy Vilas Warak. I am certain that the Rahul they keep referring to is me,' said my son to me over the phone.

It was just another day, but with that the curtains to one of the most trying phases of my life opened. For the world, it was entertainment. For me, it was nothing short of a catastrophe.

'What should I do? Pooja and Mummy are saying that I should seek your advice and go to the police. What should I do, Pops?' he asked, trying to sound normal, but I could hear the dread in his voice.

It was bizarre. Of all the cities in the world, it seemed that a terrorist called David Headley had picked this one. And then, on top of that, of all the millions of people in this teeming metropolis, he had chosen my son to befriend! I was in possibly the biggest dilemma of my life. In this world, where we keep talking about courage and duty, parents, however, are programmed to steer their offspring away from danger and to avoid risks. Don't we train our children to seek out safety, to be wary of strangers, to fasten their seat belts, and to look all over the place before crossing the road? The very thought of losing them to some careless act of theirs or someone else's haunts us day and night, and propels us to hover over them continuously.

But you are what you do, not what you say you ought to do. The whole family was being tested. Were we going to be mute spectators, or risk the public glare and perform the role that destiny seemed to have chosen for us?

The first impulse was to push away this impending tsunami that seemed to be moving steadily towards us, and keep silent. One had seen innumerable accounts of how this phobic post-26/11 public mood was propelling investigative agencies to act in the most unjust and inhuman manner towards so many innocents, and in particular to so many poor Muslim boys who were incarcerated for no real reason. Also, the thought that right-wing forces, with whom I have been fighting bitter battles, along with their plants in the media, would seize this opportunity to tear me to shreds and harm my son, was daunting to say the least. I realized only too well that this was not some television show about some unfortunate guy out there that I could switch off with the press of a button. This was real life, this was my son, and he was at the other end of the telephone line, waiting for an answer that could change his life.

I asked him a question. 'Have you done anything that you are not telling me? Because if you have, you will have to bear the consequences of your own deeds, son. But if you haven't, you have nothing to fear. Hold your head up high and go to the police.'

Before he hung up, he laughed. 'Pops, I've done nothing wrong. Trust me.'

What followed were the best of times and the worst of times. The worst because the very culture that pretended to admire and express gratitude towards the men who had sacrificed their lives in the carnage of 26/11, turned around and put these two young men in the dock. Rahul, Vilas, our family and I became the staple diet of hungry news watchers, night after torturous night. Right-wing forces combined with news channels to deliberately create suspicion around my son and demonize him. What I could never understand is how, instead of applauding these two courageous boys for helping clueless investigative agencies gain deep insights into the actions of this double agent, everyone and anyone came to the conclusion that they were guilty of treason. In fact, they were heroes. Vilas even lost his job and has not got it back to this day.

It would be fair to say that the National Investigation Agency (NIA), the Mumbai Police and the Intelligence Bureau (IB) officers behaved with tremendous dignity and applauded the boys privately if not publicly. But my so-called friends and relatives suddenly shrank into the background somewhere, fearing some kind of terrible crime was about to be uncovered. I, who had stood up for every Tom Dick and Harry, suddenly found myself alone. My brave and fiery daughter Pooja and I formed a firewall around Sunny and fought the battle on a daily basis, waiting for the tide to turn in our favour.

But they were also the best of times. Because my son and I became close to each other for the first time in our lives. He began to see that the man who had walked away in the middle of the night in 1985 had actually not gone anywhere. Ironically, all the years I had spent away, carving a name for myself, helped me to finally protect him. Because if I was not famous and a 'somebody' who was respected for speaking the truth and walking his talk, I wonder if my son would have come out of this unscathed. If he had been the son of a 'nobody', would they have looked at him in the same light? As I write this, my heart goes out to so many innocent people out there who have not been as fortunate.

In some primitive tribes, when a son came of age, he killed a wild beast to show his father that he was finally a man. To me, Rahul's willingness to bare his soul, the dignity and fearlessness with which he negotiated this terrifying phase in his life when he was accused of being a traitor by some, and his desire to give a blow-by-blow account of the whole story are signs that the boy I took out for a morning walk many summers ago had now become a man.

And this man's journey has just begun.

Mumbai   MAHESH BHATT
October 2012

INTRODUCTION

The moment of epiphany occurred as my friend Adrian Levy attacked his Zaffrani Chicken Kabab with relish. He said something that suddenly made a lot of sense.

For neophytes, Adrian and his wife Catherine Scott-Clarke are a formidable team who report on terrorism in the subcontinent, especially Pakistan. Adrian is one of a kind, having covered terrorism in Pakistan for the past twenty years. He is also the bestselling author of four non-fiction books. We were having dinner together the evening before he left for Bangkok.

I had absolutely no access to Pakistani intelligence at this point and was desperate for a glimpse of their dossiers on David Headley. I could procure the information only through the 'triangulation technique', which involves communicating through a third party, since direct communication is not possible. 'Pakistani intelligence organizations, including the Inter Services Intelligence (ISI) and Federal Investigation Agency (FIA), are a cakewalk for me, just as the Mumbai mafia is for you,' Adrian told me. Oh, what a moment!

A brave and intrepid journalist, Adrian has amazing contacts with FIA officers, something he revealed to me quite modestly. Over a period of time, he laid bare to me numerous intricate

Pakistani operations, the way they displayed remarkable sangfroid while handling Indian operations, and what they felt and discovered about David Coleman Headley, or Daood Salim Gilani.

So here I am, writing about another Daood—with a different spelling. Incidentally, if the NIA sleuths are to be believed, Headley never thought highly of Dawood Ibrahim; in fact, Headley believed that Dawood lacked dedication to the community. 'He is more of a self-obsessed businessman,' Headley told a senior NIA official, who in turn disclosed this to me.

Nevertheless, both the Big Ds have a lot in common. They had strong, authoritative, famous fathers. Mumbai Crime Branch's Head Constable Ibrahim Kaskar had tremendous clout in police circles, yet his own sons—Sabir, Dawood and Anees—went astray. Similarly, Salim Gilani was a high-ranking Pakistani diplomat, but Daood, or David, turned out to be a drug peddler and a Lashkar-e-Taiba operative.

It is difficult to analyse the two Ds from the same perspective, yet the uncanny similarities between them are stark and hard to ignore—their dysfunctional families, the widening chasm between them and their parents, their quest for normal, comfortable lives, avarice for money and power, a desperation to gain recognition in the community, and highly honed survival instincts. They also derived their first names from the same revered prophet mentioned in the Torah, the Bible and the Quran—Daood or David.

In the case of Daood Gilani or David Headley, the absence of one parent or the other at two crucial stages in life seems to have enraged the hidden demons in him. Peter Taylor, a BBC investigative journalist, observed in his remarkable book, *Talking to Terrorists*, while discussing the case of Germaine Lindsay, one of the accused in the 7/7 London bombings, 'He displayed some of the factors that are common in some, but by no means all, young Jihadis: a fractured family background, vulnerability, insecurity and alienation from mainstream society.'

At another place, Taylor says, quoting terror investigators, 'When I ask nine out of ten of the young men I work with, "Tell me about your relationship with your father", most of them say, "Well, I don't have much of a relationship with my father." So, as a result, an individual has a gap in their life in terms of who their role model is, and they search for a father figure, and in particular a senior male role model. Unless they find someone who can channel them down a very positive way and give them a sense of purpose and guidance, they are really prone to a whole range of extreme radicalisation.'

Rahul Bhatt and David Headley are classic examples of this phenomenon. In fact, Rahul Bhatt narrowly escaped becoming the next Mohammad Atta. Headley's aura, personality and charm had so influenced Rahul, who did not have a male role model in his life and had always yearned for one, that he eagerly gravitated towards him; so much so that if Headley had asked him to follow the wrong path, Rahul probably would have, no questions asked. 'Headley wanted to take me to the wild west of Pakistan, the north-western provinces, though he never revealed that he was a jehadi. But he could have slowly tried to indoctrinate me into radical ideology,' Rahul told me once.

The theme of this book might appear different from that of my previous books. But 26 November 2008 is a black Wednesday for me. I lost a friend, Anti-Terrorism Squad chief Hemant Karkare, in that terror attack. If *Black Friday* was about jehadi conspirator Tiger Memon and protégé-turned-police-witness Badshah Khan, *Headley and I* is a reprisal of the journey of Rahul Bhatt with David

Coleman Headley. I am going back along the same route as *Black Friday*, only this time, to a 'Black Wednesday'.

Headley and I, or my Black Wednesday, is a story with a similar quadrant: two men—one an outlaw and the other a helper of the law. It is the story of David Coleman Headley and Rahul Mahesh Bhatt. Two men, so different, yet so alike. They belong to fractured families, are highly intelligent and charismatic, and both are wannabe James Bonds. Headley got a high out of drugs, drug dealers, peddlers and making dangerous deals with everyone, from the Drug Enforcement Agency (DEA) to senior officials of the US Justice Department, the Lashkar-e-Taiba and top echelons of the ISI. Rahul, you will be surprised to know, has read every book available on spies, terrorism and the mafia, and has watched every movie on the subject. He could tell you the kind of pistol a particular gangster was fond of. At one point of time, he even wanted to be an official spy, working for RAW. He is fascinated with weapons and could tell you a thing or two about the latest arrivals. And, of course, he is the poster boy for bodybuilders in Mumbai.

The bond between Rahul and David was a powerful one. While Rahul saw a father figure in Headley, the latter saw Rahul only as a codename for Mumbai. Rahul had spent approximately 1,000 hours with Headley and planned to spend more, when Headley was finally busted in the US. Rahul was devastated. He had lost a father figure for the second time in his life.

Narrated in an unconventional dual narrative in first person, *Headley & I* tells the story of these two from their individual points of view, taking us into their minds, their motivations, their family backgrounds and their feelings.

I must say I tried to tell it in other formats. But I realized the impact was lost, and I wasn't satisfied with my work. While Rahul let the floodgates of his emotions open in an exhaustive narrative, Headley's story was constructed from minute details recorded in the US government files and documents after his interrogation.

PROLOGUE

It was a small room, with an exit at one end and a high, barred and grilled window at the other. The walls were a subdued metallic grey. Normally, there would be exactly four pieces of furniture in the room—a table and three chairs, all made of steel. Today, however, there were three additional chairs. Consequently, the room appeared cramped, not just with its occupants but also with a sense of strain. The one distinguishing feature in this otherwise sparse and nondescript room was a surveillance camera in one corner, high up, nearly touching the ceiling, on the wall alongside the door.

The room was similar to that seen in thousands of movies, where criminals are theatrically broken by policemen, where the age-old 'good cop–bad cop' routine is played out. But this was the real thing; this was where it all actually happened.

The two men sitting at one end of the rectangular table appeared composed. The three others, who sat across from them, were distinctly out of place, but were obviously trying their best not to show it. Conversation was strained, and after barely a few minutes of forced politeness, both parties lapsed into silence, waiting. The one thing in common between the two sets of men was that neither had any trust in the other.

Exactly at the designated time, without any preamble, the door opened and two men walked in, escorting a third between them. The group of three at the table looked up with interest.

This then was the man they had flown halfway across the world to meet.

He was casually dressed, shirt and denims visible under an orange jumpsuit, and seemed totally at ease. It was evident that this was a routine he had become used to, as he immediately walked up to the only vacant chair in the room and sat down.

The first thing that struck them was his eyes, one brown and one green. It gave him a strange other-worldly air. They had never seen a man with mismatched eyes in different colours. The man's gaze and demeanour exhibited total sangfroid. He did not betray even a hint of stress or anxiety. Neither did he evince any interest in the three strangers present in the room, almost as though he was entirely unaware that three pairs of eyes were boring holes into him.

Rahul Bhatt had told them that he was a muscular, well-built man. But this man was overweight and flaunted a prominent paunch. He seemed to have been well nourished in the US jail. Well, they were not here to assess his physical condition but to question him on his links with the Lashkar-e-Taiba.

Finally! After eight long months of negotiations between the US and Indian governments, frantic parleys and several moments of utter helplessness and frustration, they had the man in front of them. The man who was responsible for a ruthlessly executed carnage, one of the deadliest in the world during which, in the space of fifty-nine hours, 166 people were brutally killed and over 300 injured in Mumbai. The man who had made it possible for ten terrorists to come all the way by sea from Karachi and attack the economic capital of India, maiming the city and leaving a deep scar in the psyche of Mumbaikars. For eight long months, the Indian investigators had tried everything they could to find a way to get to him, and finally, here he was, sitting in front of them.

The three men knew that they did not have much time with him, maybe a week at most. It would have to count; they would have to make it count. It had taken the Indian government a lot of effort and patient dialogue to get them to where they were, and they did not intend to waste any of it.

The three men from India's National Investigation Agency (NIA) were Inspector General of Police (Internal Operations) Loknath Behera, Deputy Inspector General of Police Sajid Shapoo and Superintendent of Police Swayam Prakash Pani. They were aware that one of the most powerful men in India, Home Minister P. Chidambaram, had had to swallow his pride and personally speak to United States Attorney General Eric Holder in order for them to be allowed to interrogate the accused. A similar request had earlier been rejected by the US authorities.

The man they had come to interrogate was fifty-one-year-old David Coleman Headley, a.k.a. Daood Gilani. A man who was in every sense an American, but who worked for Pakistan and, more disturbingly, for the Lashkar-e-Taiba, and who had orchestrated the terror attacks in Mumbai on 26 November 2008. This was the shocker—the white man creating mayhem, the white man as the harbinger of terror instead of its perpetual victim. Headley was arrested on 3 October 2009 in Chicago, at the O'Hare International Airport; he was on his way to Philadelphia and from there to Pakistan. The Indian government found out about the arrest on 28 October, more than three weeks later.

Soon after the Indians heard of Headley's arrest by the US government, they sent two officers from the Intelligence Bureau to the US. They had camped in Chicago for days but had not been given access to Headley, leaving Chidambaram annoyed at the haughty attitude of the US government, which claimed to be India's partner in fighting terror.

Then ensued a hectic dialogue between the two countries. Despite the strongest of letters and alternately honeyed and caustic requests to the US, India was consistently refused access to Headley. In vain did the officials try to convince their counterparts in the West that the very fact that the attacks had taken place on Indian soil should be reason enough for them to be granted the right to question him. The only response they got was a stoic, stony silence.

This time too, it hadn't been easy. The Indian team had arrived in Chicago on 31 May but could gain access to Headley only on 3 June. And the rules for the interrogation were unambiguous. The two men from the FBI had spelt it out in precise, unwavering tones to the three NIA men. No questioning on earlier matters pertaining to the American Drug Enforcement Agency (DEA), or even regarding any previous association with the CIA or the FBI. At any moment, if they felt that the NIA was overstepping its limits, the interrogation would immediately be brought to a halt. And these were just some of the easier rules to remember.

But all that was over. The NIA had finally gained access to the man who could nail Pakistan's complicity in attempts to destabilize India; he could turn out to be the proof that India had been looking for to show the world. The three men were ready.

Headley, however, showed absolutely no signs of concern or fear. He leaned back in his chair, folded his arms and threw a lazy smile at his interrogators. There was no sign of remorse, at least none they could see. He even indicated that he was willing to answer any question that they wanted to ask him.

With a shock, the three NIA men realized that the man sitting in front of them was entirely unrepentant. That he felt no regret for the horror of 26/11, he believed in the rightness of what he had done and was convinced that the terror attacks of 26/11 were justified. Could it be that Headley was more than just someone who carried out reconnaissance missions, they wondered. Could it be, thought Behera, that the man was a jehadi? The NIA had come half expecting that it would have to grill an American who had been led astray by radical forces. That was clearly not the situation here. They realized that their questions would have to be slightly modified and even more detailed than they had originally planned to make them.

Thus began the week-long interrogation that would last over thirty hours.

ONE

As I heaved the 250-pound weight off my shoulder, the tiger on my back expanded its maw and roared. I slowly raised the weight, my eyes on the feral animal in the mirror behind me. The roar faded as I brought the weight back down. It rose again in fury as I lifted the weight, in tandem with my own screaming muscles. As I held up the weight, sweat trickled down my arms and over its feline face, which was distorted by the silent but angry roar.

I saw people in the gym looking at me curiously, watching the magnificent tiger on my back. The tattoo was very well done, and it gave me grim satisfaction to know that it expressed my feelings at that moment perfectly.

'Rahul, don't you think that's a bit too much? You could tear a ligament and be injured for life.'

I heard Vilas say the words, but they didn't really get through to me. Anything . . . anything to take my mind off the last few days.

More sweat trickled down my arms and back as I held up the weight. I looked up and glared at the man staring back at me in the mirror. Idiot! How could you have been so trusting?

No, no going back there. Have to get it out of my mind. Come on, push!

I heaved away the weight and started the squats, my third round.

In the mirror I could see Vilas standing right behind me, ready to spot as all gym trainers are trained to do. He was frowning, his whole body tense, watching my movements with a worried expression. Behind him, I saw others watching me. Almost everyone in the gym had stopped their various activities—bench presses, lateral presses, lunges, cycling, running; one guy was actually holding forty-kg weights in each hand, ready to start his shrugs but waiting to see how I would fare. Curiosity and awe were written all over their faces as they watched me at the military press.

I shut them all out. This was my world, my own hell, and none of the people here would ever know what I was going though. Only Vilas, my friend and confidante and fellow sufferer, inhabited this void in me, because he had seen what I had seen, been through some of what I had been through. And right now, he too was oblivious to everyone else. I knew he was concerned for me. My friend. Just like David.

No, don't go there. Just keep pushing.

I wasn't counting how many squats I did. I just kept pushing the weight up and down. Up and down . . . I could feel my muscles strain against the weight, the veins in the neck and shoulders throbbing, running lines down my body. It helped me to relax. It made me feel that the world would go on, that everything would be sorted out soon.

I kept looking at my reflection in the mirror. You, all of this is your fault, I told it. If only you had trusted him less.

But how could I have known? David, a terrorist? A laughable thought. How could David be a terrorist? A Pakistani terrorist? No way in hell, not the David I knew. There had to be some explanation. But no, everything pointed to that. However much I tried, I simply couldn't ignore the facts, couldn't ignore the hard evidence. How ironic that he was the one who taught me never to do that.

David Coleman Headley. The man I trusted with my life, who meant the world to me—a terrorist. Daood Gilani.

Suddenly, I couldn't come up from the squat. I felt my strength ebbing, my body starting to give way. My back and legs felt like wood, like they would never move; my neck was on fire with the strain.

Vilas, who was watching me like a hawk, noticed, and in a fraction of a second he came forward, tightly gripped both my wrists and heaved me back up. I managed to rise and replace the barbell on to its stand. With the weight gone, I felt lighter, though my mind was still in a daze.

Suddenly, through the haze, I heard cheering. Turning around, I saw that all the people who had stopped their workout to watch me were clapping. I looked at Vilas. He was watching me now, and gave me a slight smile. I too had often stopped my workout to cheer a guy on when I saw he was attempting something really difficult, something that required enormous power. After all the clapping, the guy would inevitably give an acknowledging nod to his appreciative audience.

But all I felt was a deep numbness. No feeling of achievement, no elation at the intense workout, nothing. I just nodded blankly at everyone and started towards the bench press when Vilas laid a hand on my arm.

'Dude, you've just done three sets of dead lifts of five hundred pounds,' he said quietly. 'You have gone through three sets of squats of five hundred pounds. And there was the military press with two hundred and fifty pounds. And you didn't even warm up first. That's enough for one day. Don't kill yourself.'

I wiped the sweat from my eyes. I felt a sudden rush of irrational anger towards Vilas welling up inside me, but fought it back. The man was only trying to help.

'Thanks, man. Maybe you're right. I'll go cool off,' I said, and walked towards the treadmill.

Half an hour later, I was outside the gym, Five Fitness, standing on a busy Juhu road. I decided to take a cab home to my flat in Bandra.

Flagging down a cab in Mumbai during peak hour is always an uphill task, but I was fortunate this time. I got an empty one in five minutes and was soon homebound.

Only when I had settled into the seat did I allow myself to think back to the workout. I realized that I was feeling better, because I had found the courage to face the demon that was lurking in a corner of my mind, one that I had been pointedly ignoring. I reclined and let my mind drift back to that terrible day.

It had been on the news for a while, but I didn't see it till late in the evening. I had come home at around 8.30 p.m. My mother was watching TV. As usual, she had it on a notch too loud, I've never understood why. I was just going for a shower when the name 'David Headley' caught my attention. Curious, I went to the sitting room, where Mom had just switched channels. I took the remote from her and found the earlier channel while she went to get a drink of water. At first, I was convinced it was a mistake or it was some other David Headley they were talking about. But the next moment I saw a grab of his face on the news channel Headlines Today.

My whole body went rigid. David? Arrested? Had he got into

drugs again? But no, he had told me that chapter of his life was over, that there was no way he would get back into drug dealing.

Then came the other piece of news—another guy had been arrested along with David. The name rolled off the reporter's practised tongue: 'Tahawwur Rana.'

How could David have been arrested? Maybe he was a CIA agent, an American spy on a mission to India. I told myself I would have to find out.

But the horror was just beginning.

'Both men have been charged with carrying out terror-related activities on foreign soil. They have been charged with conspiring to attack the office of the Danish newspaper *Jyllands-Posten* over its publication of cartoons of Prophet Muhammad, which had sparked widespread anger amongst Muslims. Headley had allegedly scouted out the place for a planned attack by a Pakistani terror group, allegedly the Lashkar-e-Taiba, to whom he was giving out information on the location and surroundings of the office . . .' The man's voice droned on, metallic, excited by the fact that he was the one disseminating such sensational news.

The newsreader also went on about David's role in the Mumbai attacks on 26 November 2008, and how he had conducted extended reconnaissance of south Mumbai and other places in the financial capital for the attack orchestrated by the Lashkar-e-Taiba. 'Headley also conducted a recce of Taj Mahal Hotel, Trident, Chhatrapati Shivaji Terminus . . .'

I couldn't believe it, it was so bizarre. A white man—an American at that—as a conduit for Lashkar? The source of jehadi mayhem in Mumbai? The pivot for Mumbai's bloodiest carnage? I had dealt with quite a few upsets in my life, but now my world came crashing down. This was the man I had known so well, or at least thought I had known so well! I wanted to call him Dad, something I had missed doing all my life. And they were actually calling him a terrorist!

When you hear of some horror from afar, it is easy to sympathize with it, but when it happens in front of your eyes, it takes on a whole new meaning.

To me, and to the people of Mumbai, a terrorist had always been . . . well, just that, a terrorist, a monster who killed people in cold blood in other countries or in other times. That was until 26/11. Mumbai found out the hard way what a terrorist is. Sure, there was 1993 and the 2007 serial train blasts, but there was something so completely audacious, so merciless and inhuman about the way those ten men mangled Mumbai in 2008. We found out that a terrorist is nothing but a brute personification of evil. And they were saying David was one! And that he was actually a member of the dreaded Lashkar-e-Taiba.

I couldn't think. I had to speak to someone about this, and I didn't want to worry my mother just yet. Before she came back and recognized David Headley from the one time they had met, I quickly changed the channel, gave her back the remote and went to my room. From there I called Vilas.

The poor guy, who was at a friend's place, had no inkling whatsoever. I broke it to him curtly, as briefly as I could. I told him that the man we had known and trusted had turned out to be something else entirely.

'What the fuck are you talking about, man? David? You've got to be kidding! Wait, lemme switch on the TV . . . Dude, can you just give me a minute to myself? Thanks. Yeah, Rahul. Headlines Today, right? Yeah, okay, wait . . . Oh shit!'

'Yeah,' I said. 'I wasn't kidding.'

'Shit, man! What do we do?'

I heard the panic in his voice, and tried to speak as calmly as possible. 'Don't do anything right now. Just sit tight and let me figure this out,' I told him.

Vilas took it very hard. I'd gone numb from what I'd just found out and wasn't feeling anything at all, just an emptiness. Vilas, however, got really scared. That night, he didn't even ride his motorcycle home; he took a taxi instead.

I locked myself in my room. I didn't tell my mother anything. I knew she would worry. I was torn between wanting to know more about what had happened to David and Rana, and fearing I would find out something worse. Irrationally, for a moment, I even thought of calling David.

All through the next day, Vilas tried to call me. I was too shattered to speak. I only picked up his call once to tell him that I would talk to him later, and hung up. I had to come to terms with this to some extent before I spoke to anyone, even Vilas, who was the only other person who knew what I was going through. I spent the whole of 29 and 30 October at home. I didn't go near the TV, so apprehensive was I that the channels would air news that was even more disturbing.

On 30 October, I realized I couldn't take the risk of my mother finding out on her own. I had to tell her. I knew she would freak out, start worrying terribly about what might happen to me. But the truth needed to be told.

I decided to first do something to clear my mind a little, or I'd go crazy. So, on 30 October, I called Vilas and told him I'd meet him at the gym, Five Fitness, where I usually worked out. He said he still hadn't told anyone, and I asked him to keep it that way.

I hoped the workout would help. Maybe I'd be able to forget this nightmare for just a little while. Maybe I'd be able to figure out what I should do. Should I go to the police? But what if all this was just a mistake? Then I'd be betraying David, and I don't ever betray my friends. But what if it was true?

'Where in Bandra, sir?' The taxi driver's voice jerked me back to the present. It was just past 8.30 in the evening. I directed the cabbie home, to my building, Kyle More, near Mount Mary, and paid him. I was exhausted from the workout, but my mind and soul felt fresh.

Inside the apartment, I flung my gym bag to its corner, got a cold bottle of water from the fridge, settled down in front of the widescreen TV, and switched it on. Let's see what the news channels have to say tonight, I thought.

Within minutes, I realized that the nightmare was far from over.

The man on Times Now was dramatic, in the way every news anchor is when something is turning into a big story. 'Home officials say that they have still not been able to find out the exact identity of the mysterious Rahul whose name features prominently in Headley's email correspondence with the Lashkar-e-Taiba. Sources are still speculating as to whether this Rahul is a target, and whether it could be Rahul Gandhi, or even Bollywood megastar Shah Rukh Khan, whose character in several movies was named Rahul. However, the code has still not been broken, and authorities are trying to ascertain this mysterious Rahul's identity. Home Minister P. Chidambaram, meanwhile, has dismissed the view that the mysterious Rahul is Congress General Secretary Rahul Gandhi.'

It had happened. They had figured it out, they knew I was

involved in the whole thing. But no, wait! They said they still didn't know who this Rahul was! So they were still investigating.

For the first time in my life I felt as if the ground was moving beneath me. It was eerie. The floor and walls were closing in on me. I closed my eyes. Fear had put my heart into overdrive and I could hear its loud thumping against my chest. My tongue had gone dry and I am sure if anybody had looked at me, he would have done a double-take: what the hell has happened to this guy in the space of just a few seconds! In one moment, my life had changed, forever.

My brain had shut down. Oh god, what was I going to do? I felt very alone. It was only a matter of time before they figured out who the mysterious Rahul was, and then the knives would be out for me, the media would bare its fangs and god knows whether the police would believe me.

Before they came for me, I had to do something. Damn. I could tell my mother, but I knew what she would say. I knew we would have to bring Mr Mahesh Bhatt, my so-called father, into the picture. Damn, damn, damn!

She was in the kitchen, cooking. 'Mom?' I said, standing at the entrance to the kitchen. 'There is something you should know.'

'What is it?' she said, and turned. She must have seen something in my expression, because her face became grave at once. 'What is it, what has happened?'

I told her everything: what I'd seen on TV, David's arrest, that they were saying he was a terrorist. I left out the fact that David had spoken to the LeT about me, it would serve no purpose but to make her panic. I told her that they were looking for a 'Rahul', but they didn't know who it was.

Mom's face grew more and more worried as I told her. Finally, when I stopped, she laid a hand on my arm and said, 'Beta, this is too big for us now. You know you have to go the police with it. And you have to call your dad.'

I shook off her hand. 'No! Why do I have to call him? I'll go to the cops myself, there is no need to involve him in all this. He will hog the limelight and revel in the publicity.'

'He is your father, Rahul. He must know. If there is anyone in the world who can help you now, it is your father. Regardless of what you think of him, he is the only one who can save you.'

I realized she was right. I knew that I would have to call him sooner or later. But I hated it. I hated having to call Mahesh Bhatt. Why did God always throw me at the mercy of the man whom I hated the most in this world?

TWO

'David, would you like some coffee?'

'Yes, please. Thank you.'

One of the two CIA men signalled to the camera. Within twenty seconds, there was a faint buzz outside the room, and the door opened. A man walked in with a cup of coffee in a styrofoam cup, steam rising from it. He deposited the cup in front of Headley and walked out again, closing the door behind him.

The three men from the NIA watched everything with interest. It was the same formula everywhere when it came to important prisoners. No intimidation here, no threat of a beating or a 'good cop–bad cop' routine. Those were reserved for the smaller fish and for the silver screen. It was almost as if Headley was king here, as if he was doing these men a favour by telling them what he knew. Things were no different back in his country, thought NIA chief Loknath Behera, not a little cynically.

Headley made a show of picking up the paper cup gingerly, taking care not to spill the scalding liquid, and took a sip. He closed his eyes and appeared to savour the taste of the coffee, swirling it around in his mouth. Finally, he put the cup back down, opened his eyes and looked at the three NIA men.

'So, gentlemen, what were you asking me?' he said, crossing his arms in front of his chest.

'We want to hear in your own words a little bit about your background,' said Behera, leaning forward slightly and resting his arms on the table. He looked almost hungry for the information he knew and hoped would come his way.

'Ah, yes, yes. Well, what would you like to know?'

'Everything.'

My name is Daood Gilani. Although everyone here knows me as David Coleman Headley, I acquired this name later, because it suited me and helped me in what I was doing. But I was born Daood Gilani, and that is the person I have always been.

I was born in Washington DC on 30 June 1960. My father, Sayed Salim Gilani, was a Pakistani diplomat and had been posted, at various times, in various parts of the country. His last posting was with the Voice of America in Washington. My father was not a hard man, but he believed in discipline and morality and had a strong sense of what was right and what wasn't.

My mother is Serrill Headley. She is from Maryland, and is an extraordinarily resourceful person. She is the daughter of L. Coleman Headley, a former football star. Mom was working as a secretary at the Pakistani embassy in Washington, where my father was a diplomat and her boss. That's where they met, fell in love, and got married.

But ours was not an idyllic family. Far from it. My parents slowly became disillusioned with each other, and finally, in 1999, they filed for divorce. My father then remarried, and Syeda Begum became my mother.

I have three siblings—two brothers, Hamza and Daanyal, and a sister, Sherzad.

Daanyal, my half brother, is an important man. He used to work in the public relations office of Prime Minister Yousuf Raza Gilani as a spokesperson for him. He is now Pakistan's press attaché in Beijing. And before anyone asks me, I can tell you that he had no idea of what I was doing. He was not privy to information about me; he had no inkling about my missions in Pakistan or my operations in India or other places. He really was in the dark about everything that I was doing or trying to accomplish. But we know each other well, and I have often met him during my trips to Pakistan—well, stays, as you might like to call them. He is a proud person, and a good man. Leave him out of this; he has nothing to do with this.

My sister Sherzad is a doctor. She is settled in Baltimore in the US, and is quite happily married.

I have been married four times myself. My first wife was a Canadian national and we were married in 1985. We soon divorced as we couldn't get along due to cultural differences. I married a Pakistani woman next. Shazia Gilani is my second wife. She comes from an elite Pakistani family. For more reasons than one, I shall not disclose their identities. All I shall tell you is that her father's name is Javed Ahmed. Shazia and her family have no connection with me or my activities; they never have. My third marriage was to my girlfriend of eight years—I married her in New York. Finally, I married Faiza. I don't see any reason why any of them should be dragged into this affair.

Behera clicked his tongue in exasperation and looked at one of the two CIA men, raising an eyebrow quizzically. With deliberate slowness, one of them shook his head. Damn, thought the NIA team leader, we can't even force Headley to give us more information because of these two idiots sitting here! He noticed that Headley too had observed the unemphatic but unmistakable denial, but he chose to ignore it and continue speaking.

Shazia was an exemplary woman. She gave me two sons, Hyder and Osama, and two daughters, Somaiya and Hafsa. Yes, I did name my son Osama. You may ask why, and the answer is simple. Amir Osama bin Laden is my hero. He always was and always will be, both for the person he was and for what he accomplished. Naturally, I named my son Osama.

It certainly didn't surprise any of my handlers. Oh, yes, I didn't have just one handler, I had three: one from the LeT, one from the ISI and one from the Pakistan Army.

Sajid Mir was the one from the LeT. He was an amazing man and physically one of the fittest people I have ever met. He was also a well-read person, with a razor-sharp mind and an equally sharp wit. Except once, after a very minor incident at Dubai International Airport, Sajid has never been arrested. After that incident he stopped flying internationally, even though he has several passports, one of which is actually in the name of a Christian called Masih. In fact, Sajid is one of the very few LeT people who has avoided arrest for any significant length of time.

You might have heard of jehadis who are single-mindedly focused on war against anti-Islamic elements. Sajid was not like that. His mind was like a computer, and his memory seemed inexhaustible. He soaked in information like a sponge and never forgot a thing. He knew about all that was going on in the world, and kept tabs on all international incidents. He was also frighteningly efficient when it came to thinking up strategies for an operation, and could come up with various tactics for a mission almost within minutes, sometimes even on the spur of the moment. I interacted with many people across the ranks of the LeT but I met very few who were as intelligent as Sajid. The most disconcerting thing about Sajid was that he was one of the youngest in his rank; he was far younger than me and was probably in his thirties. It says a lot about the man that he achieved what he did at such a young age.

My second handler was a retired officer from the Pakistan Army—Major Abdur Rehman Hashim, alias Pasha. He belonged to the 6th Baloch. This man was a veritable encyclopaedia when it came to explosives. He was brilliant. Like Sajid, he too was extraordinary at formulating strategies and setting up operations. And he was an expert at crafting and using explosives. I soon realized that, unlike Sajid, Pasha believed in a far more radical ideology, so much so that he didn't even mind blowing up his own countrymen. Remember all those bombings in Pakistan, in Karachi and Lahore, where hundreds of Shia Muslims perished? They were all designed and orchestrated by Pasha.

During my time with Pasha, I was introduced to another army man—Major Haroon Islam. He belonged to the 10th Punjab Regiment of the Pakistan Army.

My third handler was Major Iqbal, who was from Pakistan's secret service, the ISI. He introduced me to two other ISI officers, Major Samir Ali and Lieutenant Colonel Hamzah. However, I never found out what these two were involved in. Throughout my time in Pakistan, the only man from the ISI to whom I reported on my operations was Major Iqbal.

So, at least for me, these three—Sajid Mir, Pasha and Major Iqbal—formed the triumvirate of jehadi power in Pakistan. Of course, there were others whom I met, who were higher up in their respective groups. Some of the LeT men I met were Hafiz Saeed, Zaki-ur Rehman Lakhvi and Abu Kahafa. They were not my handlers, but I did interact with them extensively. In fact, part of my training was under Abu Kahafa, who trained many others, including several like me, who were devoted to the cause of jehad. And Kahafa was one of the few in the top echelons who planned and coordinated attacks in India.

Now, I have no idea how much you people know, but I can tell you that if you are concentrating all your efforts on the LeT, you will be wasting your time. Although the LeT is the most visible jehadi group, there are many others, of whom three are the most prominent. Actually, they all conform to the LeT in one way or another; they are all arteries of the mother group Lashkar. I will give you the lowdown on these three groups, all of which were set up with the sole intent of attacking and somehow destabilizing India. And let me tell you something: they operate in such a smart and cunning manner that, try as you might, you will never be able to completely eliminate them.

The first of these three is called the 313 Brigade. It was set up by Ilyas Kashmiri in the Federally Administered Tribal Areas (FATA) region. This group swears by the Salafi/Takfiri ideology, one of the most radical wings of Islam. They believe that they are the only genuine, pure Muslims, while the rest are all kafirs. So, if someone says that he is a born Muslim, this group will refuse to accept it and continue to treat the person as a kafir, until and unless he believes in their ideology. The 313 Brigade was named after the 313 brave Muslims whom Prophet Muhammad led to war against the infidels of Mecca. These 313 men emerged victorious in the war, and the group named themselves in their memory, as they believed that such a symbolic name would ensure victory against their enemies.

The second group is one that I think all of you will be very interested in. It is called the Jund al-Fida: the word *jund* in Arabic means army, and *fida* means sacrifice. This name was chosen by Osama bin Laden, who formed this group with the sole objective of carrying out terror operations against India and other non-Muslim countries. The group was harboured and nurtured very carefully by the Taliban and the LeT, as it was the brainchild of Osama bin Laden. I remember that throughout the eight years of my training in Pakistan, everyone treated the members and volunteers of Jund al-Fida with a lot of respect.

The third highly prominent group was code-named the Karachi Setup or the Karachi Project, and it was formed specifically to train Indian Muslim youth to attack India—I am sure you must have heard of it. The Karachi Project was the brainchild of Abdur Rehman Pasha and Colonel Shah, who was Pasha's handler in the ISI. Actually, this was something I always found intriguing—I kept wondering who these Muslim youth were. During the entire period of my training and my meetings and coordination with my Pakistani jehadi bosses, I met only one Muslim youth, Abu Azmal, who was from Maharashtra. He was twenty-eight years old, and was my partner at all the major training camps that I participated in. I heard, much later, that he had been arrested by the Anti-Terrorism Squad (ATS) of the Maharashtra government sometime in 2006 or 2007.

All these Muslim youth would be brought from India after some indoctrination or they would come to Pakistan of their own free will to join the fight against India. They would come to Pakistan via Iran or Dubai and undergo extensive training so that they could go back afterwards and fight the tyranny of the Indian government. The Karachi Project, which was a special group formed within the LeT, was entirely controlled by Sajid Mir and its operations were handled by Abu Yaqoob, who was also in charge of Lashkar's naval setup. In fact, the Karachi Project launches boys from Maharashtra and Gujarat back into India by the sea route, with the assistance of a network of fishermen. I believe it was this group that trained the ten men who attacked Mumbai on 26 November. I also heard that India's National Defence College (NDC) and Raksha Bhavan were potential targets of Pasha's setup. In fact, after a conversation with Pasha in April 2009, I realized that he was planning an attack on the NDC soon.

There was an even more specialized group within the LeT, code-named the Indian Wing. Those who made it to this group had lost a loved one—a brother or a father or a son or some other family member—to the Indian Army in Kashmir. Their motive was vengeance, and the LeT stoked their anger regularly, making sure that the fire never died in them, and that their fervour to exact revenge on the Indian military never palled.

Why did I have three handlers? That is something my interrogators will have to figure out. It is a fact that the intelligence agencies of Pakistan are far superior, better organized and coordinated than their Indian counterparts. Together, my three handlers from three different sectors could provide me with everything I might require in any situation. If I needed cash, recruits, GPS equipment, etc., it was taken care of by the ISI. If I needed any specific training, the LeT would train me. And finally, the army provided me with all the information that I needed, including charting different routes for my missions. Everybody operated on a need-to-know basis. Never, at any point in time, did the left hand know what the right hand was doing. Nobody ever knew everything.

There was something else I discovered, although I never let my handlers know that I had found out something I was probably not supposed to. The longer I interacted with my handlers, the clearer it became that each of my handlers had a handler in the ISI—which meant that the ISI was taking care of everything. All the LeT bosses that I met and worked with—Sajid, Pasha, Major Iqbal, Lakhvi—had a handler in the ISI. And I noticed that none of the LeT men liked this fact. They hated being controlled and ordered about by the government's lackeys who, they felt, did not understand or appreciate the depth of Islam. They resented the idea of having to report to someone who did not know anything about the compulsions of jehad, but they were forced to accept this arrangement as the ISI gave them the protection they needed.

THREE

My father wanted to name me Mohammed Bhatt. He actually did name me Mohammed. For a little while after I was born, that's who I was—Mohammed Bhatt.

I am a bastard child.

Let me introduce my father, Mr Mahesh Bhatt. Mr Bhatt is very proud to call himself a bastard child. Of course, he is justified in doing so, as his mother and father never got married. But despite the fact that my mother and Mr Bhatt were legally married, I have always felt like an illegitimate child. The reason is simple. Though Mr Bhatt fathered me, he never fulfilled the paternal responsibilities that come with having a child. That makes me a super bastard child.

As I grew up, my mother Kiran introduced me to the man I was supposed to call Papa. Apparently, she met my father when she was fifteen and he seventeen. It was the quintessential teenage love story.

It is said that children are able to sense where they truly belong, who truly loves them, at a very early age. I was never very attached to Mr Bhatt. And by the time I realized that the man I called Father was the man who begot me, we had drifted apart.

I realized at a very young age, maybe when I was around three or four, that my father put in only a weekly appearance in my life. By

24

the time I turned seven and was going to school regularly, his presence was even rarer, as he became busy with his own life. Later, when I had grown up, my mother told me that my father had started drifting away from her even before I was born. One reason for this was the success he was enjoying. The other was Parveen Babi.

In the days when he was still making his mark in the Hindi film industry, Mr Bhatt had many unholy alliances, all of which my mother disapproved of. For instance, he had a raging, passionate, almost public affair with Parveen Babi, one of the most beautiful women I have ever met. Though my mother was no less good-looking, after having borne a child—my sister Pooja Bhatt—and approaching middle age, it is quite possible that her charm and good looks had started to wane for Mr Bhatt. Parveen and my father clearly got on very well, which is why he started spending most of his time with her instead of with my mother.

My mother also told me that most of the time, Mr Bhatt came home drunk. My parents used to fight a lot, because of which my mother couldn't bear my father's visits, irregular as they were. She would throw him out of the house when she realized that an argument was getting out of hand. Sometimes their fights would get so completely of control that they would actually run after each other with a fork or a knife, even a spoon, enraged enough to kill each other.

My father would often bring home people like Vinod Khanna, Sujit Sen, Satyadev Dubey and Suraj Sanim, his friends from the film fraternity, sometimes as late as 3 or 3.30 a.m. He would wake up my mother at that ungodly hour and order her to make food for all of them. She never refused. She would get up and religiously cook. And after dinner, Mr Bhatt and his friends would get drunk and sleep till noon.

This continued for a while, until my mother told my father that she couldn't take it any more. Finally, they took the decision to part ways and live separately.

Things could have ended there, and I don't know what would have happened. But for some reason, my father decided to reconcile with my mother. Maybe one can attribute this to the influence of U.G. Krishnamurti. UG had apparently told him to reconcile with my mother and suggested that having another child was a way to do that. The family was complete again—my parents didn't fight as much for a while; my sister was happier, and I was born.

The moment my father found out that his wife had given birth to a baby boy, he decided to name him Mohammed, in keeping with his secular ideals. In vain did people try and reason with him to choose another name, a Hindu one. Maybe it was the consequence of his Islamic background, since he grew up under the care of a mother who was a Shia Muslim. Her name was Shirin Mohammed Ali. She belonged to Lucknow and had come to Mumbai before Independence. His father, Nana Bhai Bhatt, was a Gujarati Brahmin film producer, mostly of B-grade Bollywood movies. Despite being a Shia Muslim, his mother encouraged him to maintain the *gotra* of his father, Bhargava. I am not sure whether it was this religious duality, or simply a secular defiance against communal forces that was on his mind, but he was adamant that his son should be called Mohammed Bhatt. It was only after some neighbours from a Vaidya family intervened and reasoned strongly with him, telling him that in these times of turmoil and riots, his expression of secularism would not be appreciated, and that his son would suffer greatly for it, that he finally relented and named me Rahul Bhatt.

However, his understanding of U.G. Krishnamurti's philosophy didn't seem to translate into real life. He had fathered a son, but seemed to have no feelings for him. Throughout my childhood, as far as I can remember, I never really felt my father's presence in my life. I believe that every child finds compassion in his mother and strength and power in his father. I found a lot of compassion and unconditional love in my mother, who has remained my bulwark against the world. But whenever I needed his strength or power, my father figure was absent. So what would you call someone who has a mother but not a father? A bastard, right? I felt that I was Mahesh Bhatt's illegitimate child.

I watched my mother struggle. I watched how she took care of my sister, me, my studies, my daily activities, my home, meeting my teachers, arranging my tuitions, taking care of my clothes, my requirements, tiffin—in short, everything—as my father continued to remain absent. My mother must have come to terms with this. I remember Mr Bhatt telling her that what she was doing for Pooja and me was something every mother did for her children, and that she was not doing anything special. But he himself never contributed, unlike other fathers around him. And I felt helpless when I saw my mother's pain. Imagine that you are a kid, watching your mother suffer in front of your eyes. There is nothing you can do. There were times when she didn't eat, when she just sat staring into space. It was only with great difficulty that I could get through to her at such times, as if reaching into an endless abyss to pull her out. Mr Bhatt did that to her. Yes, my father did give my mother money regularly and did take care of our expenses to an extent, but he never satisfied my psychological and emotional needs.

I did many unusual things for a child of my age. When I was ten, I acquired my first Rambo knife. Looking back, I realize that not many boys of my age, even those who were interested in guns and weapons, would have actually acquired such a weapon. I suppose it was my immature way of trying to say to the world that it hardly mattered that I did not have a strong fatherly presence in my life, that I didn't need one.

He showered love on Pooja, though, and to be honest, I could never understand why he was so besotted with my sister and gave her so much affection while abandoning me completely. When Pooja was sixteen and I was seven years of age, my father cast her in a movie with Anupam Kher. The film was titled *Daddy* and it gave Pooja her first break. Pooja, you fit the role to a T, Mr Bhatt said, and that is why I decided to cast you in that role. The movie got a lot of critical acclaim, although I don't know how successful it was commercially. It hurt me a lot, immature child that I was, that my father always used to give so much love to Pooja but never to me.

After I turned ten, I started slipping into depression, which manifested itself in a huge craving for food. I began eating everything I could lay my hands on, be it junk food or anything remotely edible. As a result, I started putting on weight, and slowly grew to become a very fat child. By the time I turned sixteen, I had become an unusually obese and depressed boy. I spent lonely hours thinking about my father, imagining that he was around, and making up stories and movies in my mind about him. I made up movies in which he would be a perfect father to me. He would return from work and I would go up to him and demand chocolates and toys like every other normal child, and he would pat me on the head, put his hand on my shoulder or hold my hand, as if he were just another normal father. I used to feel good when I dreamt up such things.

The reality, however, was harsh. Whenever I actually met him, he was either not in his senses, or was angry or busy, or else simply not bothered about paying me any attention. I realized that he was disinterested in me and seemed to want to disassociate himself from me.

He was never around. Not when I wanted a toy, not when I wanted to play; he didn't even bother bringing me a gift on my birthday. I was nothing to him. I couldn't be angry with him, even though I could see what he had done to my mother. I wanted him, I needed him, and I was trying to love him like a son should love his father. At least he could have tried too. If he had faked some affection and attention, it would have made everything so much better. But he didn't even pretend. I sat in front of him, and felt non-existent. Gradually, I grew angry. I knew how unhappy he was making my mother. Every time he visited, it ended with my mother crying for hours. And every time I saw my mother's swollen face, her eyes red with tears, I knew that her life was coming apart. There was nothing I could do to console her, to lessen the pain and grief that her husband was causing her.

The final blow came when I had just turned sixteen. Pooja had done a nude photo shoot, wearing nothing but body paint, for the cover of *Stardust*. Suddenly, we became targets for the moral police. Activists from Hindutva groups gheraoed our building, shouting slogans; some even threw stones at our house. Finally, the police had to be called in to bring the situation under control.

Throughout this episode, Mr Bhatt was conspicuous by his absence. Of course, he gave quotes to various media houses and magazines, supporting Pooja and us, and condemning what the maniacs outside our house were doing, but not once did he actually come to the troubled area and defend his family on the ground. I was the only man around to handle the situation. Overnight, this fat, depressed kid, who was himself confused and unsure of who he was, had to become a pillar of strength for the two women in the family.

I had not had a proper childhood, and was totally unequipped to handle the situation. To top it all, even the police, who had come to restore law and order, were looking at us accusingly. Their eyes said that through Pooja we had brought this 'shame' on ourselves, and that we had only ourselves to blame. So I was thrown into a situation where, on the one hand, I had to deal with mad mischief mongers, accusing cops and the simmering tension, and on the other, I had to make sure that my family was safe. If only Pooja had thought of the repercussions before she agreed to that photo shoot!

But I can't blame her, because she was only trying to further her career. I felt very sorry for my mother, and hated the fact that she was being subjected to such embarrassment. But in that situation, at that moment when I had to let go of my boyhood and become a man overnight, it struck me that more than anything else, the most potent feeling that I experienced was one of intense hatred towards Mr Mahesh Bhatt.

He had given his approval, albeit unspoken, to Pooja's photo shoot, but had washed his hands of the whole matter afterwards. It was because of his absence and his inability to stand up for us on that fateful night that I came to hate him like I hated no one else. His absence, his partiality towards my sister, the fights that I had witnessed between him and my mother, and her swollen, tearful eyes afterwards, my sense of abandonment—and now this! My hatred of him was overwhelming, it consumed me.

FOUR

The coffee cup was empty, and it seemed that Headley was wide awake now. For the merest fraction of a second, Behera wondered what would be done with the cup, and found the answer to his unspoken question almost immediately. Without any discernible prompting from within the room, the door opened, and the man who had brought in the coffee walked in again, and like before, without uttering a single word, picked up the cup and walked out without looking at anybody, shutting the door behind him.

So this must have been a daily routine for the past eight months, thought Behera, noting that neither Headley nor either of the two CIA men had shown any change in their calm demeanour, which could only mean that they had been interrogating Headley as thoroughly as only the CIA could. It also meant, he realized, that Headley must have given the CIA a wealth of information, of which they were being allowed a glimpse of just a fraction. It angered him to see that the West was treating India with its usual arrogance and disdain, even when someone purportedly theirs had made India the victim.

But there was no time to dwell on that now. Behera quickly brought himself out of his musings and into the reality of that tiny interrogation room, where Headley continued to speak,

31

revealing more details about his earlier days and what had driven him to jehad.

My hatred towards India is very old. The antagonism has its roots in my childhood.

I grew up in Pakistan. My parents Sayed Salim Gilani and Serrill Headley had come back to Pakistan from Washington. My father was one of the elite of the country; at least two-thirds of the population would have heard of him. Because of his status, I was enrolled in one of the best schools in the country, an elite military school called Hasan Abdal Cadet College, around forty kilometres from Rawalpindi.

The college and school were named after the city, which got its name from a Sufi saint. There was a Pakistani military base in the city, and the college was also known as Cadet College because of the military training it imparted.

I was an average student. But I was very interested in sports, which was encouraged in Hasan Abdal. It was because of our common interest in sports that I made friends with Tahawwur Rana in Class 7. He too was very interested in sports, and also came from an upper-class Pakistani family. We hit it off quite quickly, and by the time we left school years later, we were close friends.

In the school, children were given military training from a very young age. But nobody was radical; nobody gave provocative speeches or propagated inflammatory ideas, not even when the 1971 war was going on and our country was fighting with our neighbour India.

But everything changed one day. And that day altered my life completely.

I was in Class 9. Pakistan was at war with India. There were bombings almost every day. That day, India bombed my school. I heard much later that the two bombs that fell on my school were not intended, but I still don't believe it. My school was hit and a portion of it was destroyed. Two people were killed, though I never found out who they were.

That day, for the first time, our teacher gave a very provocative speech against India. He explained at length about the war between the countries, and how by bombing our school, the Indians had shown that they were targeting not only military installations but civilians, and even children in schools. He said that Indians wanted Pakistanis to remain backward and uneducated, and did not want our country to prosper.

Our teacher's speech touched a raw nerve, and that was when I first experienced a feeling of intense hatred towards our neighbour. I had always thought that as neighbours we were supposed to be cordial towards each other, but that day I felt that the Indians had nefarious designs, and clearly wanted to destroy every Pakistani, including children. The seed of hatred had been sown in my mind, and slowly, with time, this hatred grew to encompass others too— kafirs as well as anyone who was against Pakistan and wanted to harm her.

I grew up normal in every respect, but with that intense hatred lodged deeply and firmly inside me. Life around me was changing too, and not for the better. My parents kept fighting, and slowly, as I grew older, I realized that the idyllic love that had brought them together had died. They were constantly at loggerheads because of the different people they were and their contrasting backgrounds—elite Pakistani and high-society American. Their cultures were vastly different, and their love couldn't bridge the yawning gap that was opening up between them. Finally they separated, and my mother went back to Chicago, heartbroken because she had to leave me behind.

By the time I turned seventeen, my education in Pakistan was over. My father had remarried, and unfortunately, I did not get along well with my stepmother. My father too had grown distant from me, and more attached to his children from his second marriage. After finishing school, I was left almost alone in Pakistan.

My neighbours had given me a sobriquet, 'gora', which was a pejorative used for Americans or Britons. Unlike the average Pakistani, I was fair-complexioned, almost like an American. I did not like the term, and thought it was humiliating. Strangely enough, the unusual fairness I initially despised gave me an advantage later in my life.

It was at this time that my mother contacted me from Chicago. She had been to a bartending school called Bryan Mawr, and had used her experience to acquire a pub on Second Street near Chestnut. She invited me to join her. 'Who knows, son, you may actually enjoy yourself more here than in Pakistan,' she told me. As there was really not much left for me in Pakistan, I decided to take her advice. At seventeen, I moved to Chicago to live with my mother.

When I arrived, I was given the reception of a prince. In fact, people there actually started calling me Prince. I saw that my mother led a very different kind of life here in Chicago from what she was used to in Pakistan. It was a very social, hectic and active life. Her business was doing very well, mostly because of her own resourcefulness. She knew exactly how to attract customers. The first thing she had done upon acquiring the pub was to rechristen it the Khyber Pass Pub. It was an exotic name, the kind she knew would automatically attract patrons.

My mother used her background as a Pakistani wife who had lived in Pakistan for many years to her advantage, and would regale people with tales and anecdotes from her past life. It helped that she was a veritable lookalike of yesteryear Hollywood actress

Rosalind Russell. She also had a memorable laugh—hearty and full throated. People came to listen to, and look at, this woman who had been through so much and had achieved such a lot, and this of course helped business. For the first time in my life, I was happy. At least one of my parents wanted me in their life; my mother, in fact, had given me the warmest welcome I could have hoped for.

But all this came at a price. After having spent most of my life in Pakistan, coming to Chicago and seeing the way my mother and the people around her lived was a severe culture shock. To be honest, most of it was due to my mother. I'd had an orthodox upbringing in Pakistan, and all my life I had seen women wearing burkhas. Now I watched my mother being friendly with nearly every stranger who came to her pub, touching people, hugging and kissing and laughing, and drinking wine and beer. It shocked me, and I felt torn between a strange revulsion and happiness at being accepted into that society.

In my heart, I wanted to go back to Pakistan, but in my mind, I knew there was nothing there for me. Moreover, I knew that my father didn't want me there. Here, on the other hand, my mother did want me to be with her, but I felt like an outsider, a misfit in the milieu and social fabric of Chicago.

As the days passed, I became increasingly reclusive. I refrained from going out much. I did not have many friends. My mother tried getting me to assist her with her business and help her out in the pub, but I couldn't. Drawing on the years she had spent in Pakistan, in a Pakistani family, she even spoke to me in Urdu, trying to coax me out of my shell and put me at ease. But it didn't work. I withdrew from the hectic social life and started spending more and more time in front of the television. My mother even enrolled me in a school called the Valley Forge Military Academy to try and help me settle in and move on in life, but it didn't help. I failed simply because of a lack of will and concentration, and couldn't last even a semester. The same thing happened when she got me into accounting classes at the Philadelphia Community College. Here too I couldn't focus, and failed to get a degree.

I wasn't a teenager any more. But I was a confused young man, still perplexed, unsure and utterly clueless about what to do with my life. My mother came to my rescue once again. She thought that if she could get me into some sort of business, it would distract me from the turmoil and confusion I was going through. She helped me set up a video store called Fliks Video in Manhattan, New York. It was a well-equipped video store, and became quite popular in the neighbourhood. I enjoyed managing that store, one, because it kept me occupied, and two, because it took me away from my mother's outrageously immodest behaviour with other people.

For a while, a couple of years maybe, I focused on the business. But whatever I did, I was still unable to fit into the American way of life. Soon, I started making the wrong kinds of friends, the kind that introduced me to dope. I started small, smoking pot. Gradually I moved on to cocaine and heroin. For someone who had never experienced such things before, and came from a background such as mine, it was hugely interesting. It provided me an escape from the real world. For a while at least I could lie back, feel my body go light and wispy, and let myself just drift away, leaving the brutal, cruel reality behind me. It felt as if I was becoming a different man. Surprisingly, the Islamic mullahs who regularly condemn liquor so vociferously had absolutely no opinion on drugs, which meant that I was not committing any sin.

By the time I turned twenty-four, I knew many people like me, who were doing drugs deliberately and happily. I also knew dealers and started making deals with them. It was time for me to move on. With the contacts I had developed, I could now procure drugs for others at a very good price.

I had always imagined that I was like James Bond—one who has brilliant contacts and can ferret out any kind of information from anybody. I threw myself into the role with full dedication. As I dealt with the drug dealers of Chicago, it dawned on me that I was quite adept at manipulating people and ensuring that they listened to what I said; I also knew that I could be charming and likeable, which helped in securing the trust of these dealers. Very soon, within a year or so, I had managed to penetrate quite deep into the trade. Drug dealing became a significant side business for me.

It was around this time that I got married for the first time. She was a Canadian, who had just graduated from the Pennsylvania State University, and was working at the Khyber Pass Pub. We married in 1985. It wasn't to be a long union, because we didn't see eye to eye on many things. For instance, she could never understand why I hated Indians so much.

The marriage came to an end soon after an argument at my video store, when I hit her, a backhand blow with my right hand. My wife complained to the police about the incident, and I was arrested for assault. However, I did not get a very long sentence. It was just after this, in 1987, that my wife and I divorced. She has since remarried and settled down in Chester County, where she works as a real-estate consultant.

But this wasn't a major setback for me. I had the video store business, and I had my own little drug trade on the side. Everything was hunky-dory, until I had my first serious run-in with the cops.

I may have thought of myself as James Bond, but nothing changed the fact that I was up against the Drug Enforcement Agency (DEA). In 1988, I was arrested in a drug bust by officers of the DEA. They told me that if I cooperated, they would show me some leniency. So I turned approver, and they made me rat on my fellow traders. Instead of being handed a fifteen-year-long sentence, I was rewarded for my cooperation with the DEA, and given a jail term of only four and a half years.

I was locked up in the Chicago State Penitentiary. At that time, it seemed like one of the biggest horrors that I had ever faced in my life. I had never been to prison before, even though I had heard people talk about it. I could never have imagined what the inside of a prison looked like. It was a revelation.

There were all kinds of people in that prison. There was a Jew who always stayed in a corner. Whenever I saw him, he appeared to be praying. I later learned that the four-foot-eleven-inch-tall man had killed six people. But in there, in prison, what seemed even more terrible was that half his face had been eaten away by cancer.

There was another man called Ayub Anwar. He was always in the gym, working out. Although he and I never interacted, I followed his example and started working out too. Soon, all the excess flab that I had was knocked off, and my body became toned and streamlined. I later learned that Ayub Anwar had killed a man in prison, inside that very gym.

But the group I was attracted to was a bunch of black men. They were Americans, but called themselves the Islamic Nation Gang. They were Christians who had very recently converted to Islam. In prisons across the US, priests and preachers are allowed inside the prison to speak and preach to the inmates. While most people around me had converted to Christianity, the blacks had chosen Islam.

The men of the Islamic Nation Gang offered namaz openly, without fear of anyone. They were such a ferocious bunch that no one opposed them or got in their way. Maybe it was because of this clout and power they wielded, or maybe it was their adherence to Islam, but I was drawn to them, and they took me in with open arms. I started joining them in offering namaz, and became close to them in the process. For the next four and a half years, I was the only white man in the otherwise all-black Islamic Nation Gang. And because I was Muslim, and more educated than they were, and had far more international exposure, having lived in Pakistan, very soon I became the leader of the gang. They started looking up to me. Life in prison became good all of a sudden; I know now that it made a man of me.

After four and a half years, I was released on parole.

FIVE

It was difficult not to be scared. Vilas and I were inside the pathharwali (stone) building, as it is known among the criminal classes, the place that instils fear in the lawless, the stone-walled second floor of the Crime Branch building in the Mumbai Police headquarters, opposite Crawford Market.

This building is where crooks are broken daily, where many innocent men too have been made scapegoats just so that the cops could cover their failures. It was almost impossible not to be afraid. The room we were in was air-conditioned, and yet we were sweating. The whole atmosphere was grim. Everyone seemed to be an enemy, and we felt we would be arrested any moment now and put behind bars.

I had been feeling very apprehensive ever since my father set up the meeting with the cops the night before. I had spent a sleepless night, and had woken up just as tense and frayed as when I went to bed.

The night before had not ended well. After my mother and Pooja had convinced me, Pooja got on her hotline with our father and explained the entire situation to him. He wasn't in town that day. The three of them argued over the pros and cons of going to the police—the entire day was spent discussing this. However, my

mother was adamant throughout, and maintained that I should go
to the cops myself.

The next day, Mr Bhatt called me. The first words he uttered
were, 'Kya hua tera yeh?'

Haltingly at first, and then almost defiantly, I told him about my
association with David Headley, and that the man in the news, the
one named Rahul that everyone was harping about, was actually
me.

'Didn't you know?' my father asked me, sounding incredulous.

'I thought he was just an American. Mujhe kaise pata hoyega ki yeh
Lashkar ka agent niklega! Mujhe thodi malum tha!' I said, a little
exasperatedly.

'Tune kuch paise liye usse?' he said. 'Ya toh koi samaan?'

I felt quite offended at this, and made it clear in my tone. He was
asking me if I had taken money or delivery of any material from
David. 'Maine kuch nahin liya hai, agar liya hota, sidha sidha bolunga
main,' I snapped at him. I hadn't taken anything.

There was a pause at the other end. Then he said, 'Thik hain. Main
Rakesh se tera appointment leta hoon, jaake unse mil lena.' Then, just as
abruptly as he had called, he hung up.

A little later, he called back as the three of us sat waiting in our
living room, the TV still on, watching a news channel. I had put the
TV on mute to drown out the constant reminder of my association
with someone I idolized. The man I looked up to as a father was
now being branded a terrorist, yet, ironically, my biological father
was the one who had always terrorized me. I was left wondering
who the real terrorist was!

'I have spoken to Rakesh Maria. He will meet you tomorrow
morning at eleven,' Mr Bhatt told me gruffly. Rakesh Maria was
Joint Commissioner, Crime Branch back then. He is now chief of
the Anti-Terrorism Squad, Maharashtra.

'Have you told him what it is about?' I asked him.

'No,' he said. 'I only told him that it has something to do with the David Headley case.'

'Very helpful of you,' I said. I knew I should thank him, show some sign of gratitude, but my dislike for him was too intense. I just wished him goodnight and hung up.

My mother was looking at me reproachfully, but I ignored it. I admired my mother for her courage. For one thing, she always insisted that I should be deferential towards Mr Mahesh Bhatt, despite everything he had done to her. And she always censured and rebuked me if I crossed the line with my father.

I looked at her with ever-increasing affection and told her and Pooja that I was tired and had to get some sleep, and before they could start counselling me on what to tell the cops, I got up and went to my room.

When I got up the next morning, the bright light of day that streamed in through the open windows did nothing to comfort me or ease the tension. And the grim, concerned faces of my mother and Pooja weren't helping at all. I felt feverish, and had already taken two Calpol tablets, a common over-the-counter painkiller, within the space of an hour. Of course, my mother kept telling me that it was not fever, I was just anxious and nervous about what would happen.

Soon, Vilas arrived, looking just as worried. In fact, he looked more frightened than I did. I had called him the previous night just after speaking to Mr Bhatt, and told him that he and I would go to the Crime Branch to tell the cops what we knew. But Vilas was too scared, and refused to meet me at the Crime Branch office. So I had asked him to come to my house, from where we would proceed to the Crime Branch together.

I took another Calpol, and without waiting any longer, we got into my car. We didn't speak much on the ride there, but I sensed that Vilas was nervous, so I tried to calm him down. 'Bro, *tune kuch galti toh nahin kiya na?*'

He looked at me pleadingly, and said, '*Tujhe malum hai maine kuch nahin kiya yaar!*'

'*Toh tension mat le. Jo poochta hai, direct jawab de aur koi panga mat le, dekhna koi mushkil nahin hoga,*' I told Vilas, feeling nowhere near as confident as I sounded.

Vilas sat back, looking a little less scared. Although I was no less frightened, I had to stay strong.

I parked the car outside the Crime Branch office; I was still feeling feverish, so I had another Calpol. Then I strode into the office of the Crime Branch. Vilas followed me, shuffling his feet.

We had only just taken a couple of steps inside when we were stopped by a couple of burly officers, pot-bellied and moustached. '*Thamba,* checking *karaitcha,*' growled a constable in Marathi, approaching from behind the desk. We waited, arms outstretched, as two men frisked us thoroughly. 'Maria *saab se milna hai,*' I told them, trying to sound brisk. 'Appointment *hai.*'

It didn't impress our friskers, though, and they carried on with their search. Finally, one of them picked up a phone and dialled a three-digit number. '*Naav kae?*' he asked me imperiously. 'Rahul Bhatt, Mahesh Bhatt ka beta,' I said, noting that this blatant name-dropping did not have the kind of softening effect on the cop that I had thought it would.

'Rahul Bhatt,' he barked into the phone. He looked at me balefully as he waited, ear to the receiver, for a sign from above. Finally, he said, '*Ho.*'

We went up the narrow flight of stairs, along long, musty corridors, right through to the office of Rakesh Maria. We waited outside while an underling went in and announced our arrival to the chief of Mumbai Police's Crime Branch. Within a minute he came back out and held the door open, indicating to us that we were to go in.

Vilas and I looked at each other and went in.

It was a huge office, designed to fill a visitor with awe and apprehension.

A huge bronze shield hung on the wall behind Rakesh Maria's high-backed chair. On it was the police emblem and motto in Sanskrit: *Sadrakshanaye khalanigrahanaye*. I later learned that it means 'for the protection of the good and destruction of evil'. On the walls were a few paintings, modern art I gathered, something that has never interested me. One corner had bookshelves with huge volumes of books on international and Indian law.

Maria was seated behind a vast C-shaped table. Two rows of chairs were placed facing him, and I inferred that these must be meant for story-hungry newshounds whom Maria summoned to press conferences, which were commonly referred to among journalists as 'Maria ka darbar'.

Vilas and I were now present in Maria ka darbar, and he had every reason to behave like a king and treat us like lowly patsies. We sat down across the table from him. He clearly had a lot of work to do, and his phones kept ringing constantly during the time we were there. His desk too was piled high with paperwork, and he had the air of a man who didn't have time to meet and talk to anyone, but was being polite since he had no choice but to do so.

'So, Rahul? Your father told me that you think you can give us some information about the David Headley case?' Maria said, leaning back in his chair, obviously not expecting much, as I could tell from his demeanour.

'Yes, sir, I do,' I said, and decided not to beat about the bush. 'You know the person named Rahul everyone is talking about, the one who was mentioned in David Headley's emails?'

'Yes?' said Maria. 'You think you can tell me something about his identity?'

'I am that Rahul, sir. I am the Rahul in the emails.'

Nervous though I was, I noted with not a little satisfaction that the half-smile on Maria's lips had disappeared and the blood had drained from his face.

'What did you say?' he asked, as if he had not heard correctly.

'*Woh Rahul main hi hoon*, sir,' I repeated. I am that Rahul.

He sat up. I could tell that his mind was working furiously on the implications of my statement. 'Okay. How exactly do you know that it is indeed you?' he asked me.

'Because I knew him,' I told him.

His jaw dropped. I could tell he was utterly taken aback by my revelation. He lost his composure for a fraction of a second, then he was in control of himself again. 'I see,' he said, and sat up. 'What can you tell me?'

Over the next half hour or so, I told Maria all that I knew about David Coleman Headley. I told him about how David and I had been very close friends, and how over the course of a year and a half we had met several times. I told him how I had helped David with his diet. And I told Maria that I had been introduced to David by my long-time friend Vilas Warak.

Which was when Maria chose to attack Vilas. 'You introduced them?' he asked Vilas sharply.

'Yes, sir.' Vilas sounded nervous as hell.

'*Kidhar mila usko?*' said Maria, even more sharply.

'*Ji* sir, Moksh gym *mein.*' Vilas was trembling now.

'*Kabhi uska ghar gaya?*'

Vilas started at Maria's harsh tone. '*N-n-n-nahin,* sir.'

'*Ghar pe nahin gaya?*' It was almost a shout this time. I realized Maria was intimidating Vilas.

'H-h-h-*haan,* sir, *gaya . . .*'

Maria frowned at the guy menacingly. '*Pehle bola nahin gaya, phir bola gaya, kaunsa hai? Sach bolo!*'

Vilas was now staring at Maria, muttering gibberish out of fright.

The cop turned to me. 'Tell your friend to tell me the truth, otherwise things will really not go well for him.'

Vilas was crying now, tears rolling down his cheeks. It was an incongruous sight—as if the incredible Hulk was sitting in front of me, crying.

'Come on, man. *Bata de abhi sahab ko jo bhi hai,*' I told Vilas. Then taking pity on him, I turned to Maria. 'Sir, I think he is too intimidated by you.'

I had read enough about crime to know that was exactly what Maria was doing. I also knew that he was not going to stop. With my support and a little bit of coaxing, and with Maria's bullying, Vilas started talking. He gave Maria everything, from his home and office addresses, the places where he had met David Headley, everything.

Finally, Maria seemed satisfied. He turned back to me and said, 'Okay, Rahul. You must realize that this is quite an important input that you have given me. I need to brief my officers and get them on this immediately. In the meantime, why don't you and Vilas wait for a while outside? Would you like something to eat or drink? Maybe coffee?'

Both of us declined his offer. I was more than happy to leave his office. My conscience was clear, my shoulders felt less heavy. As the two of us came out of Maria's office, the same underling took us to the adjoining room, where we sat quietly, waiting, not speaking.

After a while, the orderly came back and signalled to us that Maria wanted to meet us again. We went back into his office and saw that there was another man with him. Maria introduced him as Deputy Commissioner of Police (DCP) Nisar Tamboli.

Soon after, Tamboli and Vilas left on a recce of Moksh and David's address in Mumbai. I was left in the charge of ACP Ashok Durhape. I could see that the man found it hard to believe I was the Rahul the entire police force had been chasing after; he seemed a little disappointed that it hadn't turned out to be a far bigger celebrity. We started talking, and he confessed to me, after having scrutinized me from head to toe, that he too was a bodybuilder. We chatted for a while, and then he got a call, clearly with instructions about what to do with me.

Immediately after disconnecting the call, ACP Durhape said that it was time for me to leave. However, he had been instructed to take me away through the rear exit of the building. As we came out of the building, he led me to a Toyota Qualis police vehicle with tinted windows. I realized that the cops did not want the media to get a whiff of what was going on just yet.

We didn't speak much on the drive to the police club. When we reached, I saw that Vilas was already there, sitting in DCP Tamboli's car, while the cop himself was outside, speaking on the phone. ACP Durhape signalled to me to say that the day was over, and I could leave. So I got down from his car, and walked towards the DCP. The man had noticed me coming and walked forward, holding the phone.

'It's good that you are here, Rahul,' he said. 'Mr Maria is on the phone and he would like to speak with you.'

I put the phone to my ear and said hello. Maria's voice came drifting across the line. 'Rahul, don't worry. I've taken care of everything. You just make sure that you don't talk about this to anyone. I'm speaking with the people in Delhi, everything has been sorted out, and all you have to do is to make sure that your phone is switched off for the next couple of days.'

'Thank you, sir, thank you very much. But what about Vilas?'

'My words apply to both of you, Rahul, you should know that. Just lie low for a while.'

After nearly three hours of anxiety, Vilas and I left for home, less frightened than before, but aware that our interrogation was far from over.

In fact, the interrogation continued the next day. Only, this time it was not the Mumbai Police. The Intelligence Bureau (IB) dropped in, all the way from Delhi, to interrogate me.

I had been feeling feverish from even before the meeting with Rakesh Maria. It was in the same state that I opened the door that evening to two men who introduced themselves as officers from the IB. The man who was obviously in charge introduced himself as Vikram Thakur, the IB's deputy director. With him was the head of the IB's Maharashtra unit, Gopal Guru. I took an instant liking to Gopal. He struck me as a good man, just from the way he talked and behaved with me. I came to have a great deal of respect and regard for him.

Both the cops met my mother and asked her some questions, but her answers soon made them realize that she was not involved in this mess at all. They asked me all the same questions Maria had asked the previous day, and it all seemed quite cursory and lasted for not more than half an hour. In fact, Thakur even joked that had I not been ill, he would have taken me out for dinner. A typical Delhi guy.

It was over soon, but I could not shake off the feeling that had come over me after my talk with Maria. I knew that the interrogation was far from over, and Vilas and I would have to face the music again.

SIX

I was still unable to figure out why I had not been able to see
through the charming David Headley. All along, the debonair
American had managed to dupe me and fool me so convincingly. He
had clearly been using me. How could I have been so obtuse?

There was something I came back to, again and again. Without
really meaning to, I had kept referring to David as Agent Headley,
which annoyed him no end. In fact, he got upset whenever I called
him by that nickname; I, of course, had no idea how close to the
truth I was. I kept accusing him, though in jest, telling him that I
knew he was a Yankee CIA agent, and that he was in Mumbai to
snoop on us and gather intelligence on Indians. And he kept denying
this, saying that he didn't work for the Americans.

How did I not figure out that he was probably a real agent? Of
course, I could never have guessed that he was an LeT man, but he
did seem the type to be working for the CIA. I was left wondering
what else about him I did not know. I wanted to find out, I *needed* to
find out, but who would tell me?

The IB had very little information. They had tried to get to
Headley; soon after his arrest in October, two IB sleuths had been
sent to the US to find out more, as they say, straight from the
horse's mouth. But the US government had sent them back without
giving them any access to Headley.

Although Headley's activities had been confined to Mumbai for the most part—his recces and stays, the people he cultivated—Mumbai Police's Crime Branch knew very little about these, as information from the IB and the NIA was inevitably diluted by the time it trickled down and reached them—they were clearly at the very bottom of the chain.

Ultimately, I had to fall back on newspaper clippings about Headley and reports in the electronic media. I decided to talk to my journalist friends and go online and try to find out as much as I could about David Coleman Headley—or Daood Gilani, as he was being referred to again and again. The more I read, the more I realized what a murky life he had led and how little I had actually known him. He had mentioned his drug days to me, but I had no idea how deeply compromised he was.

I found out that the man had been first arrested in 1988 for dealing in drugs in Frankfurt, while he was on his way from Lahore to Philadelphia. The arrest had been made by a DEA agent who was stationed in Frankfurt and had received a timely tip-off. To me, it seemed a strange coincidence that his arrest in October—his final arrest on charges of terrorism—had also taken place while he was on his way to Philadelphia, from Chicago.

For two days after he was arrested, Headley had undergone intense interrogation. Over and over again, the DEA questioned him about his drug deals, whom he dealt with, who his customers were, who his fellow drug traders were. I read in the *Philadelphia Inquirer* that the agents had told him that he could help himself by cooperating with them, and that was the only way out for him. It didn't take Headley, then Daood Gilani, long to agree. Throughout the meeting, he was very, very quiet and very in control.

Two days later, in a sting operation at his New Street apartment,

Headley delivered some drug dealers into the hands of law enforcement officers. DEA agents had the entire apartment wired for sound and video footage. That day, Headley offered fifteen kilograms of heroin to drug dealers Richard Roundtree and Darryl 'Tank' Scoggins. The drug cache was to be hidden in suitcases with false bottoms that Scoggins had brought with him. Scoggins looked at the pile of heroin on the coffee table in the living room of Headley's apartment and said incredulously, 'Is this all ours?' He gave Headley a high five. The next moment, he was in DEA custody.

One of the articles I read gave a detailed account of Headley's career with the DEA, which, I was astounded to find, had lasted several years. So Headley had turned into a double agent, betraying his fellow drug dealers and turning them in to the DEA.

That first time, Headley's assistance to the DEA got his sentence reduced by half to about four years. After he was sentenced, the judge who was hearing the trial told Headley that he was giving him a break because of his cooperation and because he did not have an earlier record. The judge also admonished him, saying, 'It's up to you, Mr Gilani. Do what you want with your life, because you are still a young man.'

Headley had told me of that first term in prison, when he had gone in unfit and naive and had come out toned and fit. I remembered that he had mentioned some of the people he had served time with. I now realized that this was when it had happened; the anecdotes and the reminiscing were about his four-year stint in the Chicago State Penitentiary.

Headley was released from prison in 1992. He then asked the judge if he could have his passport back. It seems he wanted to go to Pakistan for an arranged marriage; in fact, that is what he told the judge in his application to be allowed to travel out of the US. Later, he did take advantage of this; his probation officer Luis Caso wrote, 'He went to Pakistan and got married again in 1999, this time to Shazia Gilani.'

But the report also said that back in 1992, Headley had trouble staying clean and flunked drug tests. In 1995, he was sent back for drug treatment and rehabilitation, and was given an additional six months in jail.

After serving time in prison for the second time, Headley managed to keep his head above water for a year or so. But not for long. The more I read about the man, the more obsessed I became with him. He never seemed to learn from his mistakes despite the punishments and imprisonments. He was clearly an astonishingly thick-skinned man.

Two years later, in 1997, Headley was arrested again for moving heroin from Pakistan to the US. This time, he was caught by the DEA while he was on his way to deliver a consignment of heroin to drug dealers in New York.

And once again, the chameleon that he was, Headley changed colours immediately, and agreed to cooperate and rat on the drug dealers. He wore a wire, and as he delivered the heroin to the hotel room, where he had set up a meeting with the dealers, DEA agents swooped down and arrested everyone present.

This time, Headley had turned on a big-shot drug dealer called James Leslie Lewis. While he was given a fifteen-month sentence, Lewis got ten years. I was stunned to read that to get such a reduced sentence, Headley not only testified against Lewis but, according to court records, he also worked for the DEA as a confidential witness, setting up at least three subsequent sting operations, by which more drug dealers were ensnared.

I experienced a new kind of emotion now. After the admiration and respect, then the subsequent shock, disbelief and sense of betrayal, I began to feel rather humiliated, and angry that I'd had all those benevolent feelings towards a man like Headley. What kind of a man was he, I wondered. He obviously had no loyalties at all, and seemed to be interested only in saving his own neck, always looking for his own convenience, his escape route out of tricky situations.

The *Philadelphia Inquirer* quoted a law enforcement officer involved in the New York heroin bust case speaking about Headley, 'It was easy for him because he was of both worlds—he was a Pakistani as well as an American.'

I also read something that made my blood boil with anger. Headley was not only a rat who sold out his fellow workers, he conned the innocent into doing illegal tasks on his behalf as well.

Barely a month had gone by after Headley had pleaded guilty to smuggling heroin into New York in 1997. According to reports maintained by the DEA, he then forced a fellow Pakistani living in New Jersey to buy heroin from him. This man, Iqram Haq, was not the most intelligent of individuals, did not speak English, and had been totally bowled over by Headley and his glib talk. The news report said that Headley had befriended him when they served time together in prison.

At the 1998 trial in New York, it was Headley's word against Haq's. The case, according to the media, was going to be an open and shut one, and everyone expected that Haq would be convicted and handed a long sentence. But justice was served. The jury acquitted Haq, providing a rare victory to a defendant who was claiming entrapment. During the trial, Sam A. Schmidt, Haq's attorney, described Headley as a common run-of-the-mill drug-dealer-cum-informant, who was caught while trying to save his own neck.

In another drug bust case in 1998, Headley worked as a confidential informant for the DEA against a man called Zahir Babur, who pleaded guilty of flying to Lahore, acquiring one kilogram of heroin there and smuggling it back to New York. The heroin was hidden inside seven books in his luggage. With Headley's inside information, the DEA arrested Babur, who was given a prison sentence of three and a half years. It was around this time, in November 1998, that Headley began serving his fifteen-month sentence at the low-security Federal Correctional Institution in Fort Dix, New Jersey.

The original sentence called for Headley to remain on probation for five years after he served his sentence, until mid-2004. But, within six months, Headley was out of jail and headed to Pakistan for a month-long trip, with the approval of a federal judge and the Department of Justice, a *Philadelphia Inquirer* report said. Furthermore, at the end of 2001, his attorney as well as the prosecutor asked the judge to end Headley's probation early. The judge agreed.

I could not believe my eyes. How could the US have been so callous as to let this man off lightly when he had been arrested twice and clearly had connections with the drug mafia?

According to Rocco Cipparone, a former federal prosecutor, in a scenario such as this, eight or nine times out of ten, the accused is certain to be cooperating with his captors, or is being rewarded for past cooperation. In fact, if he was still an informant for the DEA, it would make it even easier for everyone to grant him leniency. And if he was not on probation, he would no longer need to seek permission from the court to travel anywhere.

All this meant only one thing—that Headley was heavily supported and protected by the DEA because he was constantly helping them bust one drug deal after another, and handing them both Pakistani and American drug dealers.

After about two months of imprisonment on drug charges, Headley was back in Pakistan, this time doing more than dealing in drugs. I realized, as I continued to read, that the Headley case was just one of a number of recent cases in which Americans had been linked to terrorist acts.

Two women in Minnesota, both US citizens, had been convicted of channelling funds to a terrorist group in Somalia called al-Shabab, which was allegedly aided by the Al Qaeda. They were also charged with recruiting fighters for a terrorist cell. This was followed by several more arrests in connection with alleged terror plots in Denver, Boston and Dallas. Separately, five young Americans were arrested in December 2009 in Pakistan for planning to attack US soldiers in Afghanistan.

Luis Caso, Headley's former probation officer who was himself intrigued at the developments, was quoted in another newspaper report as saying, 'All I knew was that the DEA wanted him in Pakistan and as fast as possible, because they said they were close to making some big cases.' Clearly, I thought, Headley and his association with the DEA showed that his government ties ran far deeper than had been generally known. And all I had done was peruse news articles. God knows how much more dirt there was in the records of the US agencies dealing with him.

That Headley's cooperation was highly valued was apparent from a September 1998 letter which the prosecutor had submitted to court. The letter showed that Headley, who had admitted to distributing fifteen kilograms of heroin, had come to be considered over the years to be so 'reliable and forthcoming' that they sent him to Pakistan to 'develop intelligence on Pakistani heroin traffickers'.

However, according to Caso, the government took great pains to not reveal which agency was handling Headley, or even whether he was working for more than one agency.

Headley did not just help these DEA agents on the field by masquerading as a drug dealer himself. In that same letter, the prosecution told the court that Headley, who was facing anything between seven to nine years in prison, had become such a trusted partner for the DEA agents that he helped translate hours of tape-recorded telephone intercepts and coached drug agency investigators on how to question Pakistani suspects. In short, he had become an invaluable asset to the DEA.

Now I knew that Headley could manipulate anybody and worm his way out of any situation. If he could deceive even DEA agents by coaching them on drilling drug dealers, he could manipulate pretty much anyone.

While he was on probation, in October 2001, a woman called up the FBI, saying she used to date Headley. She told the authorities that she believed her former boyfriend was sympathetic to extremist groups in Pakistan. A senior American official later admitted that the FBI hadn't paid enough attention to this tip-off, because in those days, just a month after the 9/11 attack on the World Trade Center, the government was flooded with thousands of such calls. They merely thought that a fair number of people were using the opportunity to try and fix their enemies and settle scores, and this woman's tip-off was not to be taken seriously either.

It is unclear how widely disseminated the girlfriend's warning was, but within a month, Headley's help was enlisted, and his sentence suspended in exchange for what court records described as 'continuing cooperation'. According to a transcript of that hearing, the whole thing was a rushed affair.

Obviously, to me at least, from the little that I had found out about David Headley from the Internet, and from what I knew of him personally, the US was then, in the aftermath of the 9/11 attacks, considering 'assignments that went beyond drugs' for him. Headley helped the DEA to infiltrate the very close-knit Pakistani narcotics-dealing community in New York. He also travelled to Pakistan to gather intelligence.

After 9/11, the US was desperate to get details about terrorists and their activities, and Pakistan was on its radar. And since Headley was already their trusted confidante, who better to help gather intelligence on terrorists than him?

Incredibly, through all this, Headley maintained a string of relationships with women. This, despite the fact that he had an obvious antipathy towards so many things. In fact, his first wife had even told the police, after they had divorced, that he would get so enraged if he saw an Indian on the street that he would stop, curse at the fellow and spit on the street, and spit again.

Headley married Shazia Gilani in 1999, which was when, I remembered, he had applied to the court to be allowed to go to Pakistan for an arranged marriage. And in 2002, he married his girlfriend in New York. But apparently, he was still not satisfied. Before his visit to India, in the last week of February 2007, he got married to Faiza, a Moroccan national. She was a student at the Lahore Medical College. Apparently, he kept his other wives in the dark about her.

By then, he was already spending most of his time in Pakistan. I realized that this was when he started to change. In 2002, he was given a free US pass to travel to Pakistan as many times as he wanted, and this must have been when he started harbouring radical ideas, and fell in with the Lashkar-e-Taiba.

That must have been when he became double agent Headley.

SEVEN

The five men sat in the room, waiting for Headley. Nobody spoke. But this time, the Indians were more focused and eager to get on with their work. They hadn't slept the night before, preferring to pore over their notes. Just like before, Headley was brought in, followed by a man with a cup of coffee.

Behera had had enough of Headley's ramblings about his early life. He was here primarily to investigate the terrorist attack on Mumbai, and he was not interested in Headley's version of wrongdoings towards Pakistan.

What Behera was interested in was how the LeT fit into all this. He knew they were responsible for the attack, but how were they involved with Headley? How did a white American get access to one of the most dreaded terror organizations in the world?

As Headley started speaking again about the American way of life, the NIA team leader interrupted unceremoniously. 'Yes, Mr Headley. Thank you for your details and the background you gave us earlier on those terrorist groups in Pakistan. Can you please come to the point?'

Headley turned to Behera and gave him a winning smile. 'What would you like me to tell you? You know I'm only here to cooperate.'

Behera remained poker-faced. 'Thank you. Tell us how it all began. How you started out with the LeT.'

Headley looked up at the ceiling, as if he was trying his best to remember all that had happened ten years ago. With a visible effort, he marshalled his thoughts and started speaking.

It was in 2001 that I landed in Lahore. I had just been released from a short stint in prison, and realized, with some dismay, that even though I was in Pakistan, my own country, I was still confused about what to do next. I had already been divorced once, and had married a second time, and I was still a misfit in American society. I knew, deep within me, that my heart was more in Pakistan than in the US, even though I looked more American than anything else.

I had handed over my video store to my cousin Farid, who was looking after it and handling the business. My mother too had her hands and her life full, managing her pub in Chicago. But I was drifting.

One evening, after spending a few days wandering aimlessly about in the city, I went to pray at Qadisiyah Jamia Masjid. It is one of the biggest mosques in Pakistan, and is best known for its Salafi thought and the radical Islamic beliefs that are routinely propagated there.

My first glimpse of the mosque took me by surprise. It was heavily guarded, much more than any others I had been to in Pakistan or elsewhere. And what was even more strange, there were men holding carbines and AK-47 assault rifles, on guard at the entrance and all along the perimeter of the mosque. I told myself that it was probably because of a perceived threat against the mosque from some quarters of liberal Muslims or other enemies.

As I was coming out of the mosque after offering namaz, I saw a huge billboard right outside the mosque. The poster exhorted devotees to donate money for the cause of jehad. I was astounded at this open declaration of jehad, and the even more direct exhortation for donations. Out of admiration for the bold declaration, I decided to donate some money.

Behera interrupted Headley, his expression one of incredulity. 'It was all being done openly?'

Headley smiled. 'Yes.'

'They ask for donations and recruits openly?'

Headley nodded.

Behera was unsettled, and looked it. No wonder then, he thought, that there is such an anti-India feeling in Pakistan! Of course, not everyone would be swayed by this ideology, but there were always people who could be brainwashed and converted.

Behera shook his head, regained his composure and gestured for Headley to continue.

I called up the number that was advertised on the poster, and told the person on the phone that I wanted to donate some money. He said he would call me back. Within a minute, a fellow who introduced himself as Brother Abid called me and asked where and when he could come to collect the money. I told him to come to my house and gave him the address of the flat in which I was staying in Lahore. He thanked me and hung up.

Abid turned up at my flat an hour or so later, and I gave him Rs 50,000. He took the cash and was about to leave when he turned and gave me a quick appraising glance. He then told me that if I was interested in more than just donating money, I could come to an *ijtema* (gathering) led by Hafiz Saeed later in the evening, at a secluded spot near the mosque.

I was very interested.

That evening, I attended Hafiz Saeed's lecture. I was immensely impressed by everything he said. During the course of his speech, Hafiz Saeed quoted a hadith from *Saheeh Bukhari*, a book in which all the current and authentic traditions of Prophet Muhammad have been collected. *Saheeh Bukhari* is considered a guide for common Muslims in their day-to-day life. Hafiz Saeed explained that the money spent for the cause of jehad gives much more *sawab* (virtue) than innumerable namaz offerings in the sacred precincts of the Holy Kaaba in Mecca, the holiest of Islamic shrines, on the auspicious night of Lailatul Qadr, or the grand night.

After the lecture, Abid, who is currently based in Spain, introduced me to Hafiz Saeed himself, and we spoke for a while. Hafiz Saeed's words left an indelible impression on me. I spent the whole night thinking about what he had said. If money could indeed grant me so much sawab, why shouldn't I give more? Why shouldn't I do what he was saying, and promote the jehadi cause?

Behera interrupted Headley again. 'Mr Headley, I want to show you some photographs. Can you identify the men for me, please? Is Hafiz Saeed among them?'

He then took out a set of blown-up photographs from a brown envelope, put them on the table and slid them over to Headley, who studied each of them silently for nearly a minute, a frown on his face.

Then Behera watched as Headley correctly identified every single person in the photographs—Sajid Majid, Abdur Rehman Hashim and Abu Alqama, all hardcore LeT leaders. But Saeed wasn't among them.

'Okay, Mr Headley, now can you identify these voices for me?' Behera said, and nodded to Pani, his right-hand man.

Pani took out a small cassette player from his briefcase and pressed play. There were several voices from several recordings, all intercepted phone calls. Headley again proved supremely cooperative, and identified the voices of Abu Alqama, Sajid Majid and Abu Kahafa, as they spoke to the 26/11 Mumbai attackers.

Behera took another gamble. He loaded Google maps onto his laptop, then pushed it across the table. 'Can you locate any of your handlers' residences?' he asked, his heart racing.

With practised ease, Headley's fingers flew over the keyboard and soon, he had marked out several locations in Pakistan—the houses of Hafiz Saeed and Pasha, his own flat, and a couple of LeT safe houses.

Behera sat back. Finally, they had some hard evidence and a witness to testify that Pakistan was behind the 26/11 terror attacks. But there was still a great deal left to extract from Headley. 'Thank you,' Behera said. 'Please continue. You said you had just attended a lecture by Hafiz Saeed and were thinking of promoting the jehadi cause?'

After that, I began attending the ijtemas of Hafiz Saeed regularly, never missing any if I could help it. Slowly, as I replayed his speeches and explanations delivered in his powerful oratorical style in my head, I became aware that I was definitely moving towards the Salafi ideology. I had become totally influenced by Salafi ideas and radical Islam.

I believe I have told you this before, but just to refresh your memory, Salafi Islam is a branch of Islam practised by people who are commonly known as Wahabis in India and have an affinity towards the brand of Islam practised in Saudi Arabia. They believe that they are the original followers of Islam and all other people are kafirs who have been misguided or misled.

As I became a regular at the ijtemas, my face became known amongst the crowd. Soon, through these gatherings, I was also introduced to other stalwarts among the jehadis, people who believed in the original Islam, in the righteousness of jehad for the sake of Islam, and who wanted to avenge the injustices that had been and were still being done to Muslims around the world. For that, they reminded us, they were willing to kill. As I fell in with them and went deeper into their circles, I discovered that these men were from the Lashkar-e-Taiba.

Then, one day, at one of the gatherings, Zaki-ur Rehman Lakhvi rose to speak. I was introduced to him later that day, and I asked him about furthering my learning and fighting for the cause of jehad. But Lakhvi and others at the ijtema that day told me that I was totally ignorant and had no real knowledge of Islam. They advised me to get some kind of initial training to become a true Muslim first. I was asked to attend something called Daura-e-Amma. This is the basic orientation given to all those who are interested in joining jehadi outfits and fighting for Islam.

I spent a couple of years thus, learning namaz, being taught the various intricacies of Islam, about jehad, and a million other things I had never even heard of.

Then, when I had passed the Daura-e-Amma, I was introduced to something called Daura-e-Sufa sometime in the beginning of 2003, in Muzaffarabad, in Pakistan-occupied Kashmir (PoK). This was designed to show how our religion had been distorted and mercilessly tampered with by all and sundry across the world, and to demonstrate that most people did not follow the original, authentic Islam.

The Daura-e-Sufa lasted for only a few weeks. By then, my heart had turned completely sympathetic to the cause of jehad and the innumerable jehadis who were laying down their lives every day, so much so that I wanted to go and fight with my brethren against the enemy in Jammu and Kashmir. My blood boiled at the atrocities the ruthless Indian forces had unleashed on the Kashmiris.

I asked Hafiz Saeed if I could go to Jammu and Kashmir and join the battle with my brothers in arms. But he only told me that Lakhvi was my commander, I should consult him.

Hafiz Saeed and Zaki-ur Rehman Lakhvi both believed in jehad, but they had very different roles to play. Hafiz was known for his fiery oratory. He would use his ijtemas to convince people that theirs was the true Islam, and that everything else was a sham. Lakhvi would take over from there. He told them that jehad was the true way of life. 'If you have become a Muslim, now Islam wants your blood, Islam wants your sacrifice,' Lakhvi would say.

However, what Lakhvi told me left me disappointed. 'It isn't advisable for you to go to Kashmir, because you are too old for that kind of mission. In the war in Kashmir, we need fighters who are in their twenties, are agile and have young blood coursing through their veins. You, my friend, have already crossed your forties. We cannot allow you to go to Kashmir,' he told me.

My dream of fighting in Kashmir remained just that, a dream, although I kept thinking that someday, when I was fitter and better trained, I would convince my handlers to send me there. I told myself that someday I would go and fight side by side with my Kashmiri brothers, who have been fighting against the Indian forces.

EIGHT

I had spoken to Rakesh Maria of the Crime Branch and two officers from the IB, but I knew that the grilling was far from over. The police weren't going to let me go so easily. Maria's jurisdiction was limited to Mumbai, and this matter went a lot further. I wouldn't have been surprised if RAW had decided to land up at my doorstep.

A couple of days after our first meeting with Maria, I received a call from an officer with the Intelligence Bureau. He told me that I would have to come in for questioning again, and this time, I would have to give my statement to the NIA.

'We need to know the whole picture, Mr Bhatt,' the guy said. 'And we need to know it straight from the horse's mouth.'

'Of course,' I said. 'So I've got to go to Delhi now?' I didn't want to go to Delhi as I really didn't like the city, not after growing up in a city like Mumbai.

The man chuckled. 'No, Mr Bhatt. At least, not just yet. There's an NIA team here in the city to talk to you.'

'When do you want me to come in?'

'Tomorrow, please. Shall I send a car to pick you up?'

'No, thanks, I'll come on my own.'

He didn't insist. Instead he said, 'Please bring your friend Vilas Warak. We want to question him too.'

I said we'd both be there, wrote down the address, and hung up. Then I called Vilas and informed him that we had been summoned for questioning, this time by the NIA, and told him to come to my house the next day. 'Don't worry. They know our story now, it won't be too bad,' I said, though I wasn't feeling confident myself. Far from it.

Our destination the next day was the Police Officers' Mess at Worli. This newly constructed state-of-the-art office is located on Pochkhanwala Road in Worli. When the CBI or NIA or any other intelligence agency sends teams across to Mumbai, the officers stay here and use these offices as makeshift investigation cells.

We reached the office on the appointed date and exactly at the appointed hour: 14 December 2009, at 4.30 p.m. After we had identified ourselves at the reception, an officer named Nair called from upstairs, asking us to wait in the reception area. In less than five minutes, he came down to greet us.

We shook hands, and I introduced both Vilas and myself. Nair told us he was with the NIA and asked us if we were bodybuilders. We began chatting about exercises and workouts, and I saw Vilas visibly relaxing. I was still on my guard and kept wondering when this honeyed small talk would end and Nair would come to the point. Finally, the man at the reception signalled to Nair, and he told me that I would have to go with him to the sixth floor. I looked at Vilas. Nair told Vilas to wait at the reception for a while, as someone would be down shortly to take him for questioning too.

On the sixth floor, the lift door opened to reveal a row of rooms, five or six in all, all quite nondescript. It was to one of these rooms that I was led by Nair. There were quite a few people in the rooms we passed, seated at tables and desks and working on what seemed like mounds and mounds of papers. The moment I stepped out of the lift, I sensed a subtle change in the atmosphere, as if the usually relaxed occupants of the floor were suddenly slightly more alert. I could sense that all of them were staring at me, assessing me from inside the rooms and behind the tables. I felt like an animal that had just been brought into a zoo or a circus. All that attention made me a little self-conscious but I shrugged it off and walked ahead confidently.

Nair escorted me to one of the rooms where three very menacing-looking officers were waiting for me. One of them went to the door and closed it very pointedly and ominously. They were trying to intimidate me, and at first, I must confess, it did work. My confidence was partly shaken by their daunting demeanour.

No one spoke for a long time, and I felt myself being assessed by the interrogators. I looked at the nameplates on the uniforms of the officers and memorized their names. There was Deputy Superintendent Rajmohan from the Kerala cadre of the Indian Police Service—he was from the NIA. There was an IB officer named Radhakrishnan. The third man in the room was an officer of the rank of inspector general, who was introduced to me only as Singh. He looked extremely fit, a rarity among our law enforcers. He had a tiger moustache and sat straight-backed and stiff. He was clearly the man in charge.

Singh started to speak. He began by telling me about himself, probably to put me at ease. He said he was an IPS officer from the 1986 batch, and that he too was a fitness freak like me. 'Do you know, Rahul, I'm a marathon runner, and I run five kilometres every day,' he told me conversationally, as if we were two participants in a fitness programme.

'That's impressive, sir,' I replied.

The interrogation that followed was pretty much the same as the one conducted by Maria. The same questions—how I had met David, where I'd met him, how long I'd known him, where I'd taken him, what we did, and so on. By then, I had gone over everything so many times in my mind that I had no difficulty in answering any of the questions. I spoke for about thirty minutes, and they kept firing questions at me continuously about Headley and my association with him. Singh never interrupted me when I was replying, asking the next question only after I had finished answering the previous one. He was a good listener, and kept taking notes as I spoke.

Soon, though, he started asking me some very weird questions. 'Rahul, do you speak Arabic?' he asked.

Arabic? Me? I told him that not only did I not speak Arabic, I knew nothing about the language.

The next question was equally intriguing. 'Have you ever been to Pakistan, Rahul?'

I was flummoxed. I was a hundred per cent sure that these guys had access to my passport and visa status. All they had to do was refer to their notes and they would know. Nevertheless, I told Singh that I had never been to Pakistan.

It dawned on me that the four men were playing some kind of mind game with me. I noticed that while Singh was doing the actual questioning, Radhakrishnan was watching my reactions like a hawk. I realized later that he was probably working out some sort of a psychological profile based on my responses. I thought of Vilas down there at the reception, awaiting the same fate as I was, facing such menacing men on his own. It was all a bit unsettling.

All of a sudden, Singh again changed the subject, and asked me for some tips on fitness and on a proper diet. How should he work out? What was my specialty?

I answered all his questions patiently, giving him some tips on nutrition and some exercises and weight training that he could do.

Suddenly, while we were in the middle of fitness tips, Singh changed tracks again. 'Mr Bhatt, are you hiding anything from me? Because if you are, we will confront you with evidence and then you will have no defence left for yourself.'

He probably thought that I would be thrown by this, but I was expecting it and was ready. 'No, sir, I'm not hiding anything at all. Everything I'm telling you is the truth,' I said.

He steepled his fingers and looked hard at me. Then he said, 'Okay, I can see that you want me to believe you. Then tell me something. If you're not hiding anything, why did you refer to him as Agent Headley?'

I had already answered all the questions about why I thought Headley was an American agent and probably from the CIA. But since I was being asked again, I decided to tell him a little bit about myself. So, for the next few minutes, I told him about my interest in crime, that I loved reading mysteries and books on crime and weapons, and that I found security networks fascinating. I told him that as I kept reading up on all this, I started looking at everyone around me a little more suspiciously than usual. When Headley began to tell me about his past life, my suspicions grew.

Headley always liked to flaunt his knowledge about spy craft and espionage, and his knowledge of different kinds of weapons. He once told me that he had spent time training with the Special Security Group (SSG) of Pakistan. He knew how to operate different kinds of weapons, like the Austrian Steyr AUG, the Chinese Star pistol, the AKM, and the Heckler & Koch German rifle. He had trained to use the M-16 rifle, as well as the Glock pistol. In fact, he said he had also been trained to use an RPG, an anti-tank grenade launcher.

'So, Mr Singh, when someone tells you all these things, what do you make of it?' I said. 'He told me he was just a businessman who has an immigration office. But how does a simple businessman come by all this knowledge? And what the hell is a businessman doing getting training in so many different kinds of weapons?'

I was in full form, unloading all the information stuffed in my head. My only thought was to somehow convince these men in the room that there were a million things about David Headley that, in retrospect, didn't add up and which would lead any logical, rational man to believe that he was much more than he seemed, perhaps even a sophisticated agent.

I told Singh that Headley had once told me that he knew Ayub Afridi. 'I had never heard of this man at all!' I said. 'But Headley told me that Ayub Afridi was a hot-shot drug lord, the Pablo Escobar of Pakistan. And he told me that he knew him personally. What else would you make of him, Mr Singh?'

I paused for breath, and wondered if I should go on. Singh gestured to me to continue.

I told them about the weapons bazaar that Headley had once spoken about. He had said, while talking about Afridi, that there was such a bazaar in Peshawar, Pakistan, where one could get Uzi submachine guns cloned in Iran. Imagine! Not only did the man know what Iran was making and that such guns were being cloned, he even knew where they were making them and where they were being sold.

Headley also told me that heroin was openly sold in Pakistan and that he had some very good contacts in the drug mafia there. According to him, the entire drug belt in the Pashtun area of Pakistan was run by the heroin mafia. He once told me an anecdote about the manufacture of heroin there, which I thought I would share with Singh.

According to Headley, one of the sure-shot and most commonly adopted ways of manufacturing heroin undetected was to do it in a moving vehicle. If the vehicle is constantly on the move, it's virtually impossible to track it. So, they would carry out the entire process in a moving Toyota station wagon. The workers would climb in with all the raw materials, and the vehicle would start moving towards the drop-off point for the drugs. Along the way, the raw materials would be processed and converted into the heroin that was sold internationally. Headley said that all this was being done openly in Pakistan.

When I paused at this juncture, Singh looked at me sharply and said, 'Is there anything else that you remember, Rahul?'

'Yes. Headley said that he knew Mullah Naseem Akhundzade.'

'Who?'

I told him that I too had had trouble remembering the name, but had come up with a simple solution. 'Haramzade, Mr Singh, Haramzade!' I said.

At least, that's how I remembered the name. This man, Headley had told me, was an Afghan warlord. And without his knowledge and consent, nobody could manufacture, move or sell either drugs or weapons.

'So tell me, Mr Singh, do you blame me for thinking that Headley was an agent?' I asked. He didn't reply.

I felt exhausted, but I knew that the interrogation was not over yet. The men in the room kept asking me the same questions and I repeated everything I had said, word for word, without missing out the smallest detail. Finally, after four hours or so, when all of us were spent, we took a break.

In between, they had mentioned Vilas to me, and told me that he too was being questioned and that I should be truthful, especially if I had nothing to hide, since they would compare Vilas's statement with mine and check for any discrepancies. I later heard that Vilas had had a rough time during his interrogation, and had to endure a lot of mockery and humiliation. They kept ridiculing him for being a bodybuilder, and made him take off his shirt and pose bare-bodied.

The questioning resumed after the break, and I again repeated all that I had said before and they checked for discrepancies. They didn't find any. This time, however, they were more aggressive. For example, one seemingly innocuous question that they fired at me was actually a highly loaded one, and contained a thinly veiled threat.

'If you are telling the truth, Rahul, and if you were not involved with Headley and his terror mission, how can you explain the 240-plus phone calls that you made to him?' Singh asked me.

This was again a question with a perfectly reasonable answer, and I gave it to them.

'Sir, I have already told you that we were in close contact with each other, and kept in touch pretty much all the time. Isn't it natural that you spend a lot of time talking to a person you are close to?' I said. I added that Headley was taking steroids under my supervision, which made me responsible for his health. I had to keep a tab on his well-being.

Then came another question, which seemed to contain a veiled threat. 'How did you know about both his phones? Why did he give you both numbers?'

I again reminded my interrogators that Headley and I were friends at the time. It was quite natural for him to give me both his numbers just in case I had to call him and one of them was unreachable. 'He gave me both his numbers and I saved them without thinking twice,' I said. 'Why would I be suspicious?'

Finally, the seemingly never-ending interrogation came to an end after seven long hours, and we left the Police Officers' Mess at around 11.30 at night.

I was summoned again after two days and taken to the same room where I had been interrogated earlier, but the men in it this time were different. It was S.P. Pani of the NIA, an officer of the rank of superintendent of police, who questioned me. Pani later became the investigating officer of the 26/11 attacks and the Headley probe. There were three other south Indian officers in the room, but I could catch only two of the names—Radhakrishnan and Vijayan.

The men surrounded me as I sat down. They were obviously trying to intimidate me into making a blunder or an error or perhaps saying something that would not tally with my earlier statements. They were probably expecting that I would break down and confess to my involvement in the 26/11 attacks.

They changed their tactic of interrogation and adopted another line, which I found extremely cryptic and irritating.

'Mr Bhatt, you're so patriotic!'

They kept repeating this throughout the interrogation, until at one point, it became banal. Once, I even stopped and said, 'Yes, I am a patriot. Do you doubt my patriotism and my love for my country?'

They didn't give me a direct answer to this, nor did they relent.

This time, the interrogation was not as extensive as before, and I was allowed to leave after three hours. This time, too, they kept Vilas away from me and interrogated him in a separate room. I think the idea was to get one of us to break down and confess, but neither of us did, for the very simple reason that there was nothing for us to confess to.

We were called again after two days to give statements. This time it was only Pani who took down my statement. There were none of the theatrics of the two earlier interrogations, and Vilas later told me that he too had been treated better.

Two days later, we were called in again and made to record our statements one more time. So, in effect, I was made to give my statement four times. Each time, they asked me if I was hiding something, but I had only one answer to give, a resounding, convincing no! By that time, I was feeling as if I had spent more time with the NIA and in that interrogation room than I had spent with Headley. In fact, I later found out that they spent more time with me than the NIA team had spent with Headley when they went to Chicago.

But it seemed that the NIA was still not satisfied. Sometime in January 2010, they called me for interrogation again, this time to Delhi, where I gave my statement and was grilled for the fifth time. The NIA's Delhi office is located in the Jasola area, near the Indraprastha Apollo Hospital, on the fourth floor of the Splendour shopping mall. I found this rather weird. How could a premier investigation agency like the NIA have its office inside a shopping mall?

This time, though, it was different. The questions asked were far more cursory than before, almost as if they didn't expect my answers to be any different. Then they took me to another room where they made me listen to some intercepts of phone calls that they had acquired and asked me if I could identify the person speaking and if it was David Headley. But it wasn't, and I told them so.

My interrogation by Crime Branch chief Rakesh Maria and officers of the NIA and the IB was both exhausting and unnerving. To answer the same set of questions repeatedly for hours on end was psychologically devastating. After going through those strenuous rounds of questioning, I felt as though I was in a trance. My mother used to tell me that I was behaving like a zombie. And she wasn't wrong.

NINE

After a couple of days of interrogating David Headley, Behera thought he had more or less figured him out. He knew that Headley would tell him much of what he knew and had done, primarily because he had a boastful streak in him. All Behera had to do was egg him on. So far, the strategy was working beautifully.

'Tell me about your training, Mr Headley,' Behera said. 'You clearly had a lot of training with Lashkar-e-Taiba, and they must have trusted you a lot.'

Headley beamed. 'Yeah, they trusted me.'

'So what kind of training did you get exactly?'

After the first two preliminary stages—the Daura-e-Amma and Daura-e-Sufa—I progressed to the next. The training became much more practical, and I learned to translate my acceptance and belief in Salafi Islam and radical ideology into action.

In April 2003, I volunteered for the Daura-e-Khaassa in Muzaffarabad in Pakistan-occupied Kashmir. There were thirty or forty of us in the group that underwent the Daura-e-Khaassa training, which lasted for a full three months. During that time, we were taught the importance of being soldiers of Islam and how jehad should be the raison d'être for all Muslims.

At first, it was a little difficult for some of us to accept that we would now have to do more than just believe in Islam, that we would have to act in the name of Islam and jehad. But the one thing that some individuals in the group had trouble dealing with was the bloodshed. They kept asking themselves, and each other, and our masters and trainers and teachers, if it was acceptable to kill human beings, and if so, why.

This was what Daura-e-Khaassa was all about. The earlier Dauras were orientation programmes, this was the real induction into jehad. We were told that it was not just okay to kill others, it was actually an act of worship—it needed to be done to avenge the wrongdoings against Muslims. The LeT established this primarily by showing us very gory and violent movies about atrocities against Muslims.

We were shown one film after the other during those three months. One of those movies that I still remember vividly was the one on Babu Bajrangi and atrocities in Gujarat.

I had heard that Babu Bajrangi was a Hindu radical, belonging to the Gujarat wing of the Bajrang Dal. He was involved in killing innocent Muslims in Gujarat; he had been caught on a hidden camera saying that he didn't mind if he was hanged, but before he was, he wanted to be given a couple of days so he could go and kill as many Muslims as he could. Despite overwhelming evidence, the Gujarat state and the Indian government did not act against him.

My blood boiled as I watched the movie showing all the inhuman atrocities inflicted upon Muslims in vivid detail. They had been innocent, and had been killed without any reason, in the most brutal manner possible. My hatred for and rage at India increased manifold during those three months.

We kept thinking how helpless we all were. There we were, with the wherewithal to kill this murderer, this maniac Babu Bajrangi and all others like him, but we were not doing anything at all.

We were also shown some of the innumerable inflammatory speeches made by the Maharashtrian goondas of the Shiv Sena and their supremo Bal Thackeray. Hafiz Saeed was the one who showed us the damage that Bal Thackeray had done to the Muslim ummah. We hated the man, and watching the videos of his speeches left us feeling angry and with murder on our minds. We realized that there were so many people in India who wanted to keep Muslims underfoot, and who wouldn't mind wiping out every single Muslim from the face of the earth. And we kept watching those movies.

I know now that they were shown to us primarily to motivate us, and reassure us that there was no harm in taking up a mission in the name of jehad and Islam, and killing non-Muslims in India. And after everything that we saw on those videos, all our reservations were washed away, and we were fuelled by an unnatural, powerful rage. As it is, I had nursed a hatred against India ever since I was a child and my school had been bombed, but now, my loathing and animosity towards it were reinforced and with good reason.

Finally, after graduating from the Daura-e-Khaassa, we were taken to a mountain in Muzaffarabad. It was far removed from the hustle and bustle of the town, and very secluded. At first, I thought the next part of our training would be in a cave, as it looked like that was where we were headed. However, although it looked like a cave from outside, we soon found out that it was much more. It was a self-sustained branch of the Lashkar-e-Taiba. The sheer grandeur of the place took my breath away—it appeared to be more like a palatial fortress than anything else.

It was a safe house, and it was called Bait-ul Mujahideen, meaning the 'house of the crusaders'. Whenever mujahideens would cross over from India's Jammu and Kashmir or from Pakistan, they would be stationed here and taken care of. Here, they lived a life of luxury until they were ready to leave, or were given details of their next mission. They would then cross the border to India.

There were close to forty people in our group. There were several non-Pakistanis, including a British national and a man from New Zealand. There were different camps for these foreigners, where the usual regimen of namaz was not followed. But they were allowed to pray if they wanted to.

I also met a frogman while I was in Muzaffarabad; he was introduced to me as Abdur Rehman. He seemed to be from the Pakistan Navy.

In that Lashkar camp, Bait-ul Mujahideen, we received intensive all-round training. The emphasis was primarily on urban warfare, and we were trained in two-man, body-attack operations. We learned to cover our partners and work with them seamlessly. We were taught all kinds of urban warfare skills—two-man entry, two-man firing from cover, and covering jams and reloads. We also had situational training—stair work, hall work, combat, first aid, and even unarmed hand-to-hand combat.

We were taught to shoot with all kinds of weapons—pistols, rifles, shotguns, everything. I handled the M-16, Heckler and Koch, FNAR rifles, Steyr AUG, submachine guns and even a Dragunov sniper rifle. I was also taught how to use hand grenades and anti-personnel fragmentation grenades. But the one weapon that all of us had to master was the AK-47 and its derivatives.

I learned mainly three types of shooting. The most important was rapid-response firing, which is the most helpful in ambushes. We were also taught low-light or night shooting, and the standard fifteen-metre shot.

I mentioned the name of Abu Kahafa earlier. He was present at the safe house. He is one of the fattest fellows I've ever seen. But appearances are deceptive, as I soon found out. Despite his obesity, he was extremely fit, as strong as a bull, and had amazingly sharp reflexes. In fact, I think he was quicker than many martial arts experts. I had thought of him as just another guy in the crowd during my initial training, but I soon found out that he often masqueraded thus to spot potential candidates for recruitment.

Kahafa also trained us in unarmed combat. I went through various modes of combat with him, including hand to hand and using knives. Apart from him, there were several others who gave us weapons training, and they were all from the ISI, Pakistan's Special Security Guard, or the counter-terrorism unit of the Pakistan Army, the Zarar Company. But their identities were never revealed to us at any point of time.

We went through another Daura, called Daura-e-Ribat, meaning communication. This is a derivative of the root word *rabt*, meaning connect. Another important skill we had to learn was counter-interrogation techniques. We had to keep our minds in perfect shape in all kinds of situations so that if we were ever captured alive, we would be able to deflect the attention of our interrogators, and confuse and mislead them.

There was also a strict fitness regime that we had to stick to. Every day, we had to run five kilometres, do twenty pull-ups, thirty dips and forty push-ups, along with abdominal workouts. It was essential to be physically fit, to handle the different kinds of guns. In fact, I was also taught to handle a shotgun and an RPG, a rocket launcher. These are heavy weapons, so to carry them on the shoulder and fire them required us to be at the peak of our fitness, as well as strength.

They refused to teach me how to assemble bombs. I requested my Lashkar masters and the other trainers, but they were firm about it. So I did not get any training on assembly of explosive devices.

After many months of intensive training, our Lashkar masters took us to a place called Bay'at ul Rizwan, which refers to an incident that took place during the time of Prophet Muhammad. The new Muslims of that time had sworn allegiance to the Prophet under a tree. It is said that whoever makes this gesture of pledging allegiance to Prophet Muhammad will go to heaven. That is why it is called Bay'at ul Rizwan, meaning 'the allegiance to heaven'.

My Salafi masters said that this was a solemn moment, and that we would have to take a momentous decision that would change our lives forever. He said that paying this fealty meant taking an oath of allegiance. We would always remain loyal to jehadi ideology and support it, and never, on any account, betray the cause of jehad. That was what Bay'at meant. But there was no hesitation in any of us. All of us took the Bay'at and swore our loyalty to jehad.

By now, we looked like soldiers. We had become hardened jehadis, and were fully committed to the cause. Because of our extensive training, we had also acquired confidence in ourselves, and it showed on our faces, in our gait, the way we held ourselves, the way we talked, and in a million other ways. We were now armed and ready to strike mercilessly at the behest of our masters.

My appearance too had changed completely by this time. Not only did I not have any excess fat, I was wearing only Pathani suits and had grown a long, flowing beard, which made me look like a member of the Taliban.

One day, one of my Lashkar masters took me aside and told me that there was one more Daura that I needed to do, that everyone like me, of my calibre, had to do.

Hobnobbing with the Lashkar had awakened me to my spiritual side. But the Daura-e-Tadrib ul Muslimeen in July 2004 gave my spirituality a new momentum. This was at a seminar in Abbottabad. I am sure all of us in this room know about Abbottabad, which houses a large military base.

There were many speakers at the seminar. However, to me, the star speaker was Maulana Masood Azhar. Yes, I'm sure the name strikes a chord. It is the same Maulana Masood Azhar that the Indian government had to release in exchange for the passengers of IC-814 in Kandahar. Hearing him speak was a celestial, deeply spiritual experience. Throughout his discourse, I was riveted.

As Azhar was wrapping up his speech, he said to us that our lives had no real meaning, no real purpose, and they should be spent in the cause of jehad. From then on, I was ready to die for my Muslim brothers.

After the seminar, I approached Azhar and told him that I wanted to go to Kashmir to fight alongside my brethren. I told him that I had become leaner, fitter, was much better trained than before, and that I was totally inspired and motivated, and wanted to lay down my life for the cause of jehad and for Islam.

However, the answer was once again the same. Kashmir was a very difficult terrain, Azhar told me, for a man of my age who had already crossed forty. He tried to cheer me up by telling me that I could go anywhere else and that I should be more patient. He hinted that I might soon be given a mission to carry out in India.

In 2005, I was sent to the FATA region in Pakistan, where I met Ayub Afridi, one of the biggest and most powerful drug lords there. I once mentioned his name to Rahul Bhatt, but it was mostly to impress him. I am sure you must have heard from him, Mr Behera, so there's no need to look so surprised.

By 2005, I had finished my training and had become a full-fledged member of the LeT, a jehadi dedicated to the cause of true Islam. I was itching to start work, and was looking forward to the mission in India that I had been told might be given to me. Within a few days, I was introduced to a retired brigadier of the ISI. They never revealed his full name to me, I only knew him as Retired Brigadier Riyaz.

Riyaz lived in a palatial house in Muzaffarabad, reminiscent of all those palaces that people see in movies and photographs. There were times when I was summoned to the house along with Zaki, one of my LeT masters. It was then that I realized the equation between Pakistan's ISI and the Lashkar—they were like master and subordinate. Zaki, who was a top figure in the LeT, the man in charge of all operations, was just a subservient servant in front of Brigadier Riyaz. He never disagreed with or questioned what Riyaz said, he always nodded and agreed, even if he did not like what he was hearing. I had by that time lived for years with Zaki and I knew that he did not approve of everything that Riyaz said. But the lines of power were extremely well defined. Because it was Riyaz giving the orders, Zaki would do whatever he was asked to do, without any questions.

I figured out that Riyaz was not the only man in the ISI who was dealing with our LeT handlers. Like him, Major Iqbal too was a very powerful and influential figure. His man in the LeT was Hafiz Saeed. Similarly, Major Samir handled biggies like Abu Kahafa, Sajid Mir and others.

It was a strange marriage, and I knew that the LeT despised it. To them, jehad was most important. But the ISI were really not interested in jehad. They were only interested in developing and executing strategies to destabilize India. And I knew that Zaki and the others felt their ISI superiors did not know or understand Islam as well as they did, nor did they believe as strongly in the true Islam and the Salafi ideology. But their hands were tied. The LeT could not survive without the ISI's protection, and for that, they had to comply with the ISI's directives. All my Lashkar masters listened to their ISI masters.

Finally, the ISI masters decided that I was ready for jehad, and my first mission. But they told me that there was one crucial thing I had to do first. I had to go back to the US and change my name. I was still Daood Gilani, and a Daood Gilani flying to and fro between Pakistan and other countries would get noticed, especially in the aftermath of 9/11. I was instructed to choose a name that would not raise any suspicion.

Sometime in September 2005, I called my attorney, Donald Drumpf, and told him that I wanted to change my name. He was surprised, but I told him that I had grown tired of Daood Gilani and the consequent persecution, and wanted to change my name to one that would sound as if it belonged to a white American. He believed what I said.

Finally, though my social security number remained the same, I changed my name to David Coleman Headley, using my mother's middle and last names.

At last, I was ready. This was the first time I was leaving the country on a mission, and I was leaving it a new man, as David Coleman Headley. After all those years of nursing my hatred, it was only fitting that my first mission was going to be in and against India.

TEN

Given what I now know of David Headley, it may sound surprising if I say that at times I am still unable to figure out who is more evil of the two—David Headley or my own father.

The two men treated and cheated me in a similar manner. David evoked love and affection in me, and behaved as a father would with his grown-up son. Yet, he ditched me. He had been using me all along to get information and to perform reconnaissance missions for the LeT. At the end of the day, he cheated me. Just like Mr Bhatt had done. Mr Bhatt too had ignored me, his own son, and cut me out of his life. He didn't help me when I needed him the most, and he wasn't around when I required his support and strength to lean on.

Even after all that has happened, when I know the kind of man David is and the sort of person Mr Bhatt is, I keep oscillating between these conflicting emotions for the two father figures in my life. I don't know which of them is better and I suspect that this is one puzzle I will never be able to solve.

This may seem somewhat unfair to Mr Bhatt. Even though he was non-existent throughout my childhood, I cannot get over some of the fond memories associated with him from the time when I was just coming out of my teens. Those memories make me very happy, but at times they also fill me with bitterness.

The first time I felt I really bonded with my father came about quite accidentally. I had just turned twenty, and was finally feeling more of a man.

When I turned sixteen, I had decided that I had to do something about my obesity. Yes, I was a chubby, lovable boy, everyone's teddy bear, but there were so many things I was missing out on. I saw the other kids around me, hanging out and going to movies and dates. I remember envying them, but till I was sixteen, I never really thought of changing myself.

After my sixteenth birthday, something changed within me. It wasn't any particular event that influenced me or an epiphany that I had. I got up one day and decided that I was done with the way I was living, the way I was spending my days, the way I looked, my habits, my eating disorders, everything—I decided to take charge of my life.

I started working out, trying to put my life in order by first getting my body in shape. Gradually, I started shedding all the fat that I had accumulated over the years of depression and the periods of sadness and melancholy caused by my dysfunctional family and by Mr Mahesh Bhatt.

By the time I was seventeen, I was slowly working towards building a fitter body. Finally, by nineteen, I was absolutely fit and trim, and there was not an ounce of extra fat on my body. All it had taken was long hours of walking. I spent almost all my spare time, after school and college, walking. It helped enormously, and I lost four kilograms in the first month itself.

I now decided to take my fitness to the next level. I started with weight training, building up muscle after having toned my body. I enrolled for K11 training under fitness trainer Kaizzad Capadia and by the time I was twenty, I had completed the training. Then I started working as a fitness instructor at a gym for a salary of Rs 10,000 a month. It had been quite a challenge, and I was proud of what I had achieved—going from an obese teenager to a fitness consultant in five years.

Life was looking up for me when, out of the blue, Pooja asked me if I wanted to take a couple of weeks off from my busy schedule and travel to Himachal Pradesh.

Pooja was making her first film, *Paap*, which she was both directing and producing, and the location was Spiti, in Himachal Pradesh. On Pooja's invitation, I took leave from my job and joined the crew. Initially, I decided that I would tag along with Pooja and not spend too much time with Mr Bhatt, who was also present as he had written the core theme of the movie and was helping Pooja with her directorial debut.

By a twist of fate, it so happened that when we arrived at the hotel, I found that I would have to share a room with Mr Bhatt. My plan of avoiding any kind of confrontation with my father came undone, and I steeled myself for an unpleasant time ahead.

I was wrong.

In that room, where I spent around two months with my biological father, I had the chance of observing him very closely. I realized that beneath the cold exterior, he was actually a very nice person. I feel sheepish admitting this now, but it was during that time that I found out that he had many good qualities in him, some latent, most invisible to a growing child yearning for a father. I realized that he was a very intelligent man, and wise.

Many a time during those two months, I found myself wondering where this man had been all my life. And I didn't have an answer. I didn't know why I'd had to wait so long to discover that there was a side to Mr Mahesh Bhatt which made him, or would have made him, a fantastic and exemplary father. I was privy to a part of him that had been hitherto concealed from me—he was so much more caring, and so much more affectionate than I had known him to be. I even remember wishing that he would hug me or ruffle my hair or something, although he never did so. Maybe he just wasn't that sort of a person. But when he called my name, I detected a certain pride in his voice, and whenever he looked at me, I saw his eyes betray a love that I hadn't seen earlier.

There were many other things, little things, almost inconsequential in the grand scheme of this world, that my father did for me during our stay in Spiti. He made it a point that we should have breakfast together. There were a few times when I had a late night and, consequently, a late morning, and I was surprised to see him waiting at the breakfast table for me to join him. There were even a couple of times when he did not eat his lunch until he had made sure that I had eaten something. I remember, once, being out quite late at night and returning to our room to find that he was still awake, having decided to stay up for me.

Those two months were like a dream, and I didn't even realize how swiftly they passed me by.

Pooja was mostly busy with the production work of *Paap*. The movie had big stars like John Abraham and Udita Goswami. The plot revolved around the relationship of a young girl, who is waiting to be initiated into nunhood in a Buddhist monastery, with a police officer. The girl, Goswami's character, had run away from the law with the help of the officer, played by Abraham, and had taken refuge in the mountains.

As I watched the movie unfold in front of my eyes, I saw that my father was very good at portraying a woman's sexuality. He had captured perfectly the sort of relationship a man was likely to have with a woman who is very open about her own sexuality. As he was working on the film and helping Pooja with the direction, I noticed, for the first time, this new side to my father—Mr Mahesh Bhatt the director—and I appreciated it. I was proud of the fact that there were very few directors who could have thought up and executed an idea like my father's. Earlier, I had seen only the work of Raj Kapoor and Feroz Khan and thought they were among the precious few who were good with such themes. Now I felt that my father had trumped them. I don't know if Mr Bhatt will like being compared to these legends, but all directors don't have the eye and imagination to look at a woman and be able to portray her the way my father did. Udita Goswami was portrayed in the movie like a houri from heaven!

My father and I never sat and had long talks for hours on end. I don't think he can ever be that kind of a man with me. But we did talk, and during some of these conversations, I received some genuinely good advice from him.

One day, we were getting ready to turn in for the night after dinner when we got talking. After a while, the conversation veered towards my career and how I had turned my life around from an obese child to a fitness trainer.

My father looked at me and said, 'Rahul, if you want to look at your past, you have only two choices. You can be a victim or a survivor. Either you can be affected by everything you remember and you can curse me and blame me for abandoning you. You can keep wallowing in that kind of self-pity throughout your life. You can share the grief and the depression you went through with your girlfriend, who might lend you a sympathetic shoulder and may even offer to sleep with you. This will probably help you to get by life for a few years. But you cannot live and thrive as a victim forever. There will come a time when people will become tired of you. They will look at you and think of you as a complaining man whom they have to tolerate, but not for long. You cannot wear the tag of a victim throughout your life; you cannot remain a martyr. Sympathy is not permanent, my son.'

I watched him speak, and I knew that he meant what he was saying. I realized that he was trying to show me a better way to live my life. At that moment, he was trying to be a better father than he had been before.

'The other choice that you have in life is to look at it and treat the past as the past and not let it affect your present and future. What's done is done, Rahul. Everything that has happened is now a thing of the past, and since you can't change it, all you can do is to improve your present and make your future even better. You need to take charge of your life, and you will see the difference almost immediately. People will then look at you as a confident man, someone who is willing to change his life, not shying away from taking on anything despite all the challenges and problems,' he told me.

My father then gave me his own example—his own life while he was growing up. He said, 'Rahul, you may not appreciate this or even know, but we are very similar people. I was an illegitimate child, something I am not ashamed of admitting to the world. My father abandoned me, and I didn't have a good start in life either. You know that pit, that abyss you were in? Well, I was there too, but I realized that I could not remain in it for long and suffer, I could not be like that forever. I knew that I would have to change my life and the only way I could ensure that was by changing myself, by taking the situation and my life into my own hands.'

I understood that my father wanted me to learn from him and

become aware that my life was not how it appeared to me, it was and could be a lot better. I grasped a lot of what he was saying, and I was happy that we were talking at such a personal level. I nodded, indicating that I understood what he was telling me, and I told myself that I would try to put into practice what he was trying to teach me.

We didn't speak about it afterwards, but I knew that my father and I had made a connection. Though it had come nearly two decades too late, I guess it was better late than never.

Our trip came to an end soon, and we were all packing up to leave. That was when my father came up to me and said that he would launch me in a movie.

I expressed my eagerness at his idea.

'What movie is this?' I asked him.

'Well, I am thinking of calling it *The Blue Film*,' he said.

I was stunned. The fact that it sounded like a pornographic flick, the very idea of being part of a movie called *The Blue Film* was abhorrent. I just couldn't see how I could make my debut in such a movie.

I expressed my reservations to my father. 'How can you think that I would want to act in such a movie?' I asked him in dismay.

He then narrated the movie's plot to me. It would be a take on the porn industry and how the passionate, innocent lovemaking of a young man and a woman is filmed secretly and misused by people in the porn industry and sold in the market for a price to perverts. The woman is later kidnapped and killed. During his search for her, the man unearths the activities of the country's flourishing porn industry.

But I couldn't do it and I told my father. That was when my father said something else that I will never forget.

He said, 'Rahul, people in Bollywood have lost entire fortunes because of son-stroke.'

Seeing my blank expression, he went on, 'Look at big shots like Rajendra Kumar and Dev Anand. Both these men are stalwarts in their field, both tried to promote their sons, and both suffered heavily. Even Feroz Khan suffered quite a lot while trying to promote his son Fardeen. Rahul, I am a businessman, and I know how the system works and what sells in the movie industry. I am telling you, as a father to his son, man to man. I know that *The Blue Film* will work for you. Why are you assuming that it won't? Why are you so against the idea of working in this movie?'

As I still couldn't come to terms with the idea, my father gave up trying to convince me.

Mr Bhatt went on to make the movie. It was renamed *Kalyug* and starred Kunal Khemu in the role that was offered to me. The movie was a success. It was with a lot of disappointment and hurt that I realized that my father, the perfect businessman, had gone ahead with the movie without me. What hurt the most was that when I had expressed my reservations about it, he had not mentioned anything about changing the title of the movie. But much later, while he was shooting for it, he changed the title to *Kalyug*, which he thought would be more suitable. He could have changed the name when he had proposed the idea to me and put my fears to rest. But he didn't. Too bad. Even though I did what he had asked me to do and put it behind me, it still hurts.

My father likes to show off. For instance, in *Bigg Boss Season Five*, he had absolutely no inhibitions about offering a role to porn star Sunny Leone, even going to the extent of placing his hand on her head affectionately, like a father might do. He had always had issues with treating me like a son and ensuring that I got a foothold in the movie industry. I know he will say that Sunny did not cash in on a personal tragedy to become a porn star, that she's not doing it because she's been forced into it, or because someone had held a gun to her head. She is doing it of her own volition and she's proud of what she is doing.

My father probably wanted me to let bygones be bygones and look towards the future. I don't know how he can live with the past, but the sensitive, emotional man I am, I don't think I will be able to do it.

My father didn't pressurize me into starring in *The Blue Film*, and seemed to have agreed with my decision to stay away from the project. I think he was really keen to launch me in that movie, but he respected my decision. I told him that I would wait for another break, another good movie that he might think of casting me in. Years went by, but a second offer from my father never came.

It was my sister Pooja who gave me a shot at Bollywood. By 2001-2002, Pooja had started producing movies. It was around this time that she came to me and offered me a role in a movie that was to be called *The Suicide Bomber*.

By then, the 9/11 attack had happened, and the world had changed, pretty much for the worse, I think. There was an anti-Muslim feeling everywhere, even in Bollywood. Films that appeared to be sympathetic to Muslims or to terrorists and tried to analyse their motives, the angst or the compulsion of Muslims that made them take to terrorism, bombed at the box office.

One of these movies was *Dhokha*, starring Kashmiri actor Muzammil Ibrahim and Tulip Joshi. In the film, Muzammil is a police officer who does not know that his wife Tulip is a Kashmiri militant, a suicide bomber. When she dies in a suicide bombing, he realizes why she had taken to terrorism and why Muslims are forced into terrorism and that they don't do it by choice. The movie had bombed so badly that, in Pooja's words, the only one who came to watch was a crow.

This deterred producers from making a movie called *Suicide Bomber*, which was based on a similar premise and would have been sympathetic towards the cause of suicide bombers and terrorists. As my father put it, 'Even the miyan populace from Bhendi Bazaar does not want to see such movies.'

So the movie was shelved and my second chance at a foray into Bollywood was lost.

I finally made peace with the fact that my father couldn't do anything about my career, though if he really wanted to, he could have given me the push every newcomer needs. Look at Kunal Khemu, who has found a place in the industry thanks to Mr Bhatt. Think of Emraan Hashmi. My father is single-handedly responsible for making him the star that he is today. Why can't Mr Bhatt show the same faith in me? Even my sister! She too was given a break in his movies, and my father later on consistently ensured that in many of his movies like *Daddy, Dil Hai Ki Maanta Nahiin, Sadak, Junoon* and many others, my sister figured prominently. Why couldn't he pay the same attention to his own son?

My mom asked him once whether he was averse to casting me in any of his movies because he was scared that I may not be able to act. To this, he had said insolently, 'I can direct even a stone; absolute nobodies have turned into stars. I have no fear.'

So, am I worse than a stone, a nobody? Am I perhaps not really dear to him? Or does he hold a grudge against me because I turned him down once?

ELEVEN

I was no longer Daood Gilani. That man, that identity, existed only in my mind, and in the minds of the people I was closest to—my friends in Pakistan. I was now David Coleman Headley. As an American, I hoped to have access to a lot more things than I had as Daood Gilani. I could use the identity of a white American to my advantage; in fact, even my friends would benefit from it.

I was now ready, trained and mentally prepared, to visit India to conduct recces for the purpose of jehad. I promised myself that I would do a brilliant job, and do it in such a way that every Muslim in the world, especially my Pakistani masters, would be happy and pleased with me.

I had grown to admire the LeT, which had such a fantastic setup, and whose reach and logistics were simply amazing. I found more proof of this very soon. The LeT men had delved into my background, using all the information I had given them, and had found out about my school friend Tahawwur Rana. I don't know how they managed to do it, but one day, Sajid Mir and Major Iqbal came to me and told me that they had contacted Rana and that he was on board; Rana had agreed to help us by providing some much-needed cover.

By then, that is September 2005, Rana had, with a man called Raymond Sanders, established a flourishing business called First

World Immigration Services Inc. in Chicago's Devon Avenue. They provided papers and documents and helped people in other countries, primarily in the Indian subcontinent, to immigrate to the US for a fee. Their office was in a predominantly Asian area in Chicago, and they were doing very well. Rana was not an American but a Canadian national. Over and above that, he was a Pakistani, and this is what the LeT leveraged to get him over to their side.

In the interrogation room, his face not betraying any of his thoughts, Behera made a mental note of this. According to David Headley, Tahawwur Rana was part of the conspiracy and had been as instrumental in executing the Mumbai attack as David himself. But Behera was not prepared to blindly believe everything that this self-assured man in front of them said.

Of course, he told himself, this did not mean that Rana was innocent of everything. Oh no! But it did mean that the LeT may have used a lot of pressure on Rana. Maybe they threatened to kill his family in Pakistan, or maybe they said that it wouldn't be too difficult for Rana to help them. But all this was speculation. Right now, Behera knew that David Headley's words were far more important.

My Lashkar handlers told Rana that all he would have to do was to provide finance and cover to me. Rana knew that of all the things they could have asked him to do, this was by far the least dangerous. All he would have to do was to maintain that I was a partner in his immigration business and that I was helping him expand his business in Mumbai. He might have to send me some money from time to time, and he did that too, once, when I had to collect it from a bank near the Trident Hotel.

Rana's involvement provided me with a failsafe alibi. If I was ever picked up by the Indian police, and grilled on why I was visiting India so frequently and making video recordings, all I would have to say was that I was a tourist who had just opened an immigration office in Mumbai and needed to establish my business. The videos were also for this purpose. It was the perfect cover. But it almost came to nothing because of a near-fatal error.

Rana had already got my papers in order and they had been processed. He had applied for a visa to the Indian embassy, and it was not long before I had it in my hand. I was ready to go to India—to Mumbai.

Surprisingly, there were quite a few errors in my passport and visa that nobody noticed, certainly not the Indian agencies. My father's name was not mentioned in the passport, and the visa in the name of David Coleman Headley had the father's name as Salim Gilani. But nobody questioned this. That's why I say that Indians are chutiyas.

Despite himself, Behera's jaw dropped. Until now, Headley had been speaking in flawless American English. But hearing the swear word in Hindi, Behera couldn't but be surprised. He didn't need to look at his colleagues to know that they were as shocked as he was.

'Do you know what that word means, Mr Headley?' Behera asked.

Headley laughed. 'Of course I know what it means! I am a Pakistani, don't forget. I speak Hindi and Urdu, and I know all

kinds of expletives in these languages. I don't know why you
are surprised.'

Behera had regained his composure by now. He nodded
and motioned to Headley to continue.

My social security number was the same as before. The number on
the passport was the same as the number that had been given to
Daood Gilani. The Indians would have spotted this had they cross-
checked the information. But they never did, and I was welcomed
into India with open, unsuspecting arms.

Mumbai was chosen as my destination after a lot of discussion.
The other cities that were considered were Kolkata, Delhi,
Bangalore, Pune, Nagpur, Ahmedabad and Hyderabad, but in the
end, the financial capital of India won as our primary target. Crippling
Mumbai would have a far greater impact.

I landed at Mumbai's Chhatrapati Shivaji International Airport
on 14 September 2006. Rana had arranged for me to be picked up
by a man called Bashir, who was one of his contacts in Mumbai.
Rana subsequently got Bashir to go to the US. I later learned that
Bashir was deported back to India a few months after he landed in
the US because his documents were not in order.

Bashir drove me to south Mumbai, to Hotel Outram near
Churchgate. It was a semi-luxurious hotel meant for budget
travellers. Mr Kripalani, the owner, was a very nice guy. I stayed
there and got my money changed from US dollars to Indian rupees
by a waiter called Abdullah. Everyone at the hotel was very helpful.
Mr and Mrs Kripalani were hospitality personified.

I had been instructed not to use laptops or any personal electronic
items that might be traced back to me or, worse, to the Lashkar-e-
Taiba in Pakistan. So, on my very first day in Mumbai, I went in

search of a public Internet café. I found one, called Reliance Cyber Café, near Churchgate, near the hotel, and started writing emails to Tahawwur Rana and my Lashkar masters. I was supposed to send all my findings through emails to rare.layman@gmail.com, which was my reporting email address, and to Sajid Mir as well as Major Iqbal. My own email was ranger1david@yahoo.com. I have always believed that the email user ID shouldn't be so simple that it can be traced just by running unsophisticated search programmes. Also, intelligence agencies would be hard-pressed to find out what I was reporting about and who I was emailing, especially if they didn't know the email addresses.

I stayed in India till 14 December 2006. During this trip, I made several rounds of Mumbai, conducting recces of various places like the Mantralaya and the Gateway of India. I even went to the Taj Mahal Hotel and the Trident Hotel. I had never been to the city before, and I found it bustling with life and energy. I wondered what would happen if we Pakistanis were successful in bombing it and causing major havoc. The thought was invigorating.

I returned to the US via Dubai after this first trip. Soon after, on 21 February 2007, I made a second trip to India, following the instructions of my LeT masters. This time, too, I checked into the same place, Hotel Outram, and stayed till 15 March. I again conducted recces of as many places as I could think of, to try and identify potential targets for the LeT. By now, I knew a lot more about the city and how it worked. I decided that the best course of action would be to befriend people and make some contacts. It would also help to have a local show me around the city.

I had no idea how I would casually approach and befriend people, but acting on instructions, I set up an office in Tardeo AC Market, by the name of First World Immigration. This completed the cover that Rana had provided me with. I also hired a secretary whose name was Mahrukh Bharucha.

I then decided to join a gym. From my prison days, I had learned that gyms are a great place to meet and make friends. So I went looking for decent gymnasiums and found one by the name of Moksh Wellness quite close to my office. The word 'moksh' means salvation. Chutiya Indians! They think that a gym can help you attain salvation!

I heard that the gym belonged to a celebrity, Pritish Nandy. This could come in handy. I could introduce myself as someone who worked out in Pritish Nandy's gym. It would surely break the ice and help strike up a conversation. So I went to the gym one day and told them that I wanted to join. They were very eager; after all, I was a white man wanting to sign up as a member. It is typical for the white man to be accorded all courtesies.

While I was filling up forms and completing the formalities, the man at the counter asked me for a photograph. I told him that I didn't have one, wondering what would happen next. I was surprised to find that he didn't insist on one. It's quite clear, isn't it? You can get away with anything in India. Had it been the US or any other country, they would never have allowed anyone to join a gym, or any other institution for that matter, without a photograph, especially if you were a foreigner.

I divided my time between my reconnaissance missions and my workouts. Soon, I was a known face at the gym; I could tell that all the instructors liked me and knew that I liked working out. One of those instructors was a man called Vilas Warak.

Vilas was the first person in Mumbai that I managed to befriend. Very soon, we became good friends. He was a very sincere and happy-go-lucky sort of person, and was also very helpful. He was serious about bodybuilding. He once told me that he had participated in some bodybuilding competition and won a major title. I was appropriately impressed, which I saw he liked. As I continued to work out, I kept a watch on him and how he dealt with other customers. I realized that he was really good at his job.

One day, while we were idly chatting as I was working out, I found out that he was a Shiv Sainik. Shiv Sena! Memories from my training stirred in my head as I remembered the videos I had seen, and I could feel the rage welling up in me. I knew that my job might become slightly easier if I cultivated him as a friend. I could find out more about the Sena, and maybe they would become one of the targets.

I started taking a keen interest in Vilas. Soon, our friendship expanded beyond the gym, and we were going out to coffee shops, where we would talk about a lot of things. He was delighted at my interest in the Shiv Sena, and I found out a lot about his party from him. I thought that if I cultivated him in the right manner, maybe I would be able to work my way through to Bal Thackeray. If it was up to me, I would make sure that the Sena's headquarters were bombed.

When my Pakistani handlers found out about my new friend through my regular reports via email, they were very excited, and I was informed that I should continue to cultivate Vilas Warak.

One day, I escorted Vilas to a bodybuilding competition. I picked him up and we went to Shivaji Mandir. These Indians have a temple for everybody! Apart from their innumerable major gods and goddesses and all kinds of deities, they have even set up a temple for a Maratha warrior. Left to myself, I would have bombed each and every one of these temples.

The temple brought to mind another video that I had been shown in which hordes of bearded, saffron-clad sadhus stood on some bridge in Varanasi. It was a perfect example of how misguided the Indians are. I told myself that if an explosion could be orchestrated at one of these crowded places in Varanasi, it would cause maximum impact across the world.

The venue was extremely crowded by the time Vilas and I reached. At first we mingled with the crowd and Vilas introduced me to some people; I noticed that I was the only white man present. I watched everything around me, though the function itself was very boring and extremely badly organized.

It was at this event that something happened to make my job much more exciting and potentially far-reaching. Vilas introduced me to a young man called Rahul Bhatt. He was the son of Mahesh Bhatt, one of India's most famous film directors, and known to be sympathetic to Muslims. Rahul seemed to be a very nice guy, a young chap of around twenty-three or twenty-four. It was apparently he who had organized tickets for the event for Vilas and me. He sounded very sincere and very interested in me. I shook hands with him warmly, and I could tell that he appreciated my strong grip; his too was very strong. We hit it off with each other almost immediately.

That night, I went back to my hotel and called Tahawwur Rana to report my findings to him. It had been decided that I would not call Pakistan from India, as my handlers had told me that all phone lines between India and Pakistan were under surveillance. So I would only email them, using as cryptic a language as possible to avoid any slip-ups. Since this could be quite tedious, I would also call Rana directly and report to him in words that were far clearer and more precise. Calling the US was less of a risk than calling Pakistan. Rana would then pass on all that I had said to Sajid Mir and Major Iqbal and relay their instructions back to me. I remember him always referring to Major Iqbal as *balaa*, meaning 'calamity' in Urdu.

The biggest problem I had during this Mumbai trip was that I was forced to talk to Rana in English. He and I had grown up together and always used to speak to each other in Urdu or Punjabi, which are colourful languages. But now, we spoke in English and that too very formally. We even referred to each other as Mr Rana and Mr Headley. It was quite jarring and sometimes very irritating, but I had to stick to it in case the Indians were listening in.

I left Mumbai on 15 March 2007 and went to Lahore via Dubai. My masters were making sure that there were no links between me and Pakistan, nothing to make the Indians suspicious. I stayed in Lahore for five days, during which I met Sajid Mir a couple of times.

Sajid was very happy with my report, and he especially liked two things: that I was trying to gain access to the Shiv Sena and that I had met Rahul Bhatt. He underlined the importance of developing my relationships with Vilas Warak and Rahul Bhatt, because of their links to the Shiv Sena and to Bollywood.

I returned to India on 20 March 2007, armed with similar objectives as before, as well as new ones. In keeping with Sajid's instructions, I decided to take my friendship with Rahul Bhatt a step forward. Rahul, I realized, was not a very smart guy, more the sensitive type. I told him that I was excited to have met him, and would love to know more about Bollywood. I also told him and Vilas that I would like to visit the Shiv Sena Bhavan if possible.

I had found two targets, and was getting closer to them.

But my masters had more than just Mumbai in mind. They also wanted me to scour for targets in Delhi. So, in September 2007, I made a trip to Delhi, and from there I went to Pushkar.

Pushkar is a place near Ajmer in Rajasthan where a lot of foreigners tend to converge. It wasn't exactly the urbane India I had seen until then—it had more of a hippie atmosphere, where one got to see and mingle with Europeans and Christians and foreigners. Often, they were high on drugs.

I went around Pushkar, recording and photographing extensively, and made a mental note that it would definitely have to be one of our targets. If a bomb could somehow be exploded here, there would be a lot of foreign casualties. It wouldn't be too difficult, for the security setup was not as elaborate as in Mumbai. Finally, when I was convinced that I had done all I could in Pushkar and recorded enough material on my camera, I went back to Delhi.

In Delhi, I travelled all over town looking for targets. I had visited Manali earlier and drawn up a map showing Jewish centres there, complete with detailed locations and coordinates and the security arrangements in place. I went to the most famous spots in Delhi, Rajghat and India Gate being two of them. I even went to check out 10, Janpath, which is the official residence of Sonia Gandhi, president of the Indian National Congress.

Acting on orders, I went to the National Defence College in New Delhi and conducted a reconnaissance of the place. However, since it was very well protected and monitored, I couldn't do any videography there.

I did not stay in Delhi for more than a day—I did not like the city at all. After finishing my recce in the Indian capital, I left for Mumbai that same evening.

TWELVE

My meeting with David Coleman Headley at Shivaji Mandir is a blur in my mind.

Vilas had called me earlier in the day and told me that he was bringing a friend to an event we were to attend that evening. He asked me if I would buy tickets for them, as they were running a little late.

I had the tickets ready and was waiting for them with my friends when they arrived. Vilas introduced David and me, and told me that they had met at the gym where Vilas worked as an instructor. The first thing that struck me was David's eyes: one was brown and one green. I had never met anyone with mismatched eyes before. I later found out that it wasn't as uncommon as I'd thought it to be. In fact, some famous people like David Bowie, Kiefer Sutherland and Christopher Walken have a similar condition, which is known in medical terminology as heterochromia iridum, where one iris is a different colour from the other. It is often a genetic abnormality. But seeing David, how could I have known at the time that the man had two very different kinds of genes in him, with a Pakistani-Punjabi father and an American mother?

When Vilas introduced us, David said, 'Hey, what's up?'

He had a friendly voice, and as he spoke, he stuck his hand out.

We shook hands, and I was impressed by his strong, confident grip. David was wearing dark glasses, which he took off later, a cap and a grey T-shirt and jeans. He was holding a digital camera in his left hand, which I assumed he was using to take pictures of Mumbai, like any other tourist. I thought David looked familiar, and then I realized why. He looked like a more handsome version of Steven Seagal, the Hollywood actor.

My first proper meeting with David—and the second time I met him—was on a sunny Sunday afternoon at the Barista on Chapel Road in the suburb of Bandra. It is a two-minute walk from where I live. A few days after our first meeting, Vilas had called me and asked if I would speak to David. He said that David was training with him and had expressed a desire to meet a nutrition expert who could help him with sports nutrition. Naturally, I was the guy.

When I reached Barista, Vilas and David had already arrived and were seated at a table. I got a good look at David this time. He was a very impressive-looking man. At 6'2", in his mid to late forties, David towered over almost everybody else in the café. He was a broad-shouldered Caucasian with a ponytail. But I was again struck by what I think is the most unique and defining feature of David Headley—his eyes, each a different colour.

I ordered some black coffee, the favourite drink of bodybuilders. Being a diuretic, black coffee reduces water retention and is hence considered a fat burner. Caffeine is also known to be good for the nervous system. In the course of the conversation, David told me that he was fond of bhel puri, chaat masala and pani puri. It was the first time I had seen an American talk about spicy Indian food with such gusto.

After some chit-chat, David asked my advice on nutrition. I questioned him about the sort of food he was having, and realized that his diet was deficient in protein. I told him how to increase his protein intake by consuming more natural food and taking dietary supplements. We were done after forty-five minutes, and David actually offered to pay me a consultation fee. But I declined, as he had come through a good friend, and we shook hands formally before leaving.

'We should meet up again sometime,' David told me as he sat pillion behind Vilas on his bike.

'Yeah, sure,' I said.

Our third meeting, after a couple of weeks, was at a place called Gondola in Pali Naka, again on a Sunday afternoon, around 1 p.m., over lunch. I finally summoned up the courage to ask David what he did for a living. He told me that he was an immigration lawyer and that he helped people from India and Pakistan immigrate to Canada and the US for a fee.

It was an enjoyable lunch, after which we parted ways. But this time, David and I exchanged cell phone numbers. Since he was using two cell phones, he gave me both numbers, and told me that I could call on any one of them at any time. We kept in touch after this.

We met again—the fourth meeting—after two weeks. Meanwhile, we had kept in touch through telephone calls and SMS. This time we met at a PVR multiplex in Juhu, where a film called *Vantage Point* was being screened. *Vantage Point* revolved around an assassination attempt on the US president, and it starred Dennis Quaid as a secret agent trying to protect the president. After the movie, we went for lunch to a place called Govinda, which is near the Iskcon Temple. As always happens after you watch a movie, we fell to talking about the plot and the characters and how the movie played out, and I realized that both David and I were huge action-movie buffs. We talked about the security lapses shown in the movie, and about everything else that the director had got wrong. David explained these things to me with quite a flourish, and amazed me with his knowledge of security and the way he analysed the film.

As we were finishing lunch, David asked me if Vilas and I wanted to move to Canada or the US. Seeing my puzzled face, he explained that people in the fitness industry do very well professionally in those countries, and he suggested that we should migrate there as well. I took his suggestion pretty much at face value, as I thought he was trying to be nice, but I didn't think much about it.

We didn't meet for a long time after that, for nearly four months. We kept in touch though, and he told me that he was travelling to Pakistan and the US, and that he would touch base with me when he returned to India.

We met for the fifth time at a place called Indigo Deli in Colaba. I picked up David and Vilas from the hotel where David was staying, and we drove to the restaurant, where Headley treated us to a dish called Philadelphia cheese steak. David said that his work often took him to Philadelphia and Chicago, and that he had family in both these states. Ironically, he said that the Philly cheese steak in this south Mumbai restaurant was much tastier than the cheese steak in Philadelphia itself! It became our favourite dish and Indigo Deli our favourite hangout.

It was at this meeting that we came to know of David's intricate knowledge of weaponry. He regaled us with sparkling insights into ambushes and raids and security operations throughout the world. He spoke of intelligence agencies and about how they carried out international espionage and about the security apparatus used all over the world. He told us many things about counterinsurgency operations, weapons and explosives, frisking procedures and counter-interrogation techniques.

I was intrigued and, for the first time, I suspected that he was not what he said he was. I told him that he should get into executive protection, since it was a growing, profitable business in all developed and developing countries. But David just laughed it off. When he saw that I was serious about it, he said that he would speak to some of his friends in the US who were already in the business.

After this, I began referring to David as Agent Headley. David despised being called 'Agent' and tried to convince me not to do so. But I continued to annoy him with it, and even mentioned it in subsequent emails. I later learned that he had asked Vilas a couple of times to tell me not to call him that.

Between meetings, we stayed in touch, and he often asked me how my foray into Bollywood was coming along. I had told him once that I aspired to be an actor. But whenever he asked me about my first film, I could never give a concrete answer.

After this, we met at a gym called Five Fitness in Juhu, which is where I work out. I was already running late, so when David and Vilas arrived, I called them upstairs to my flat. They came up, and I introduced David to my mother. He offered her a polite, courteous hello.

During that brief stopover at my flat, we told him that my sister had recently adopted a German Shepherd puppy as a pet. Again David displayed his knowledge about security issues and told us that American law enforcement agencies tended to use Belgian shepherds as sniffer dogs, since the breed had a far superior sense of smell than other dogs. He never ceased to amaze me with his knowledge.

We then went to the gym, all three of us, and had a macho workout session, during which David worked on the cross trainer.

After this, there was a gap of around six weeks before we met again. This time, Vilas, David and I met at the Sea Lounge restaurant inside the Taj in Colaba.

The restaurant was David's idea. We ran up a hefty bill, and even though Vilas and I offered to go Dutch on it, David refused to listen to us, and insisted on paying the entire bill himself, using his American Express credit card.

I vividly remember this meeting, because until then I had thought that David and Vilas were very good friends, so much so that Vilas used to often joke with him, saying 'we are brothers from another mother'. David would always laugh at this, but on that day Vilas crossed all limits of decency with him.

The moment we sat down at our table, Vilas said, '*Yeh behenchod ka bill toh bahut aane wala hai. Dekh le madarchod ki kya haalat hogi!*'

David kept a straight face, eating his sandwich and fries. I glared at Vilas, trying to tell him that he shouldn't behave in such a manner, and that even the other guests might get offended. But he didn't stop.

Throughout the meal, Vilas kept using expletives liberally and I was constantly glancing at David, trying to gauge if he had picked up any gaalis on the streets of Mumbai. But he remained poker-faced and did not react at all, as if he had not followed anything that Vilas said. He kept at his meal, laughing and joking with us and enjoying the food. Once, he excused himself from the table, saying he had forgotten something. He was back within ten minutes.

When the bill finally came, we saw that it was over Rs 4,500. When he saw this, Vilas said mockingly, '*Abey madarchod, itna kam khilaya aur itna bill dikhaya! Saale, humko chutiya bana rahe hain kya!*'

I looked at David, feeling very embarrassed. I was fervently hoping that people wouldn't notice, because we would be in big trouble if anyone came up to us and raised an objection to the abuses that Vilas was hurling at David. More importantly, I hoped David did not understand what Vilas was saying.

I know for a fact that the first thing many foreigners learn when they come to Mumbai is street slang. I remember that when a friend of mine had come to Mumbai with his American wife, the first thing she had wanted to learn was a gaali straight off the streets of Mumbai. And having learned one, she went up to the bus conductor in a BEST bus they were travelling on, and said, 'Behenchod, come and take the money!' The people in the bus were left gaping. David, however, gave no indication of being able to make out what Vilas was saying and remained unaffected. Little did I know then that he was actually a Pakistani who knew flawless Hindi and Urdu!

The Sea Lounge meeting was a memorable one for more than one reason, but I'll come to that later.

The three of us met again sometime during the monsoon, three or four weeks later, and by then, David and I had become very good friends. We kept talking to each other. I shared many things about my life that I don't talk about with anyone I am not close to, and he was always a sympathetic listener. He and I developed a bond, which I suspected went deeper and was more meaningful than the relationship he had with Vilas. We talked about all kinds of things—crime and criminals, drug lords, security measures, military training in Pakistan—the list was endless.

From our very first meeting, he impressed me thoroughly with his intelligence. I told myself, 'He's my kinda guy! I like the way he talks, his personality and his approach to things.' Just one glance was enough to see that he could charm his way through almost anything. Every time he walked into a room, one couldn't help but notice this big six-foot, broad-shouldered, white, handsome Yank. There was something riveting about him and his smile, I don't quite know what, it was beyond my comprehension.

I often called him David Armani because of the kind of clothes and accessories he wore. It started with his Armani clothing, which he said was tailored for him at the designer's biggest store in Manhattan. He told us that it was the same store from where Bollywood biggies like Amitabh Bachchan and Sanjay Dutt bought their suits. He was probably trying to connect with me, assuming that being an Indian and with a close Bollywood association, I would be swept off my feet by this information.

David always wore a Rolex Submariner, a brand famously preferred by drug lords and gangsters. I am not saying that I assumed he was one, but strangely, in my mind, he fit perfectly the image of *The Godfather*.

As we met frequently, I came to know that David was supremely vain. He took pride in his looks, was in love with the glint in his eyes and his beauty creams, and was terrified at the thought of going bald. He was an extrovert and extremely good at impersonating people. I also saw that he had a way with women. There was something about him that made women love him. He seemed genuinely appreciative of beauty and exercised his charm on pretty young things. He definitely had taste, be it in women or his only poison, Dom Perignon, or in his love for money and luxury.

David used to say that he loved guns and girls. He often told me that he wasn't a philanderer or a frivolous sort of man, and was always extremely respectful towards women. However, I could not fathom his reasoning, and felt that he had loyalty issues. After all, he had three wives!

David Coleman Headley

A page from Headley's passport

An open invitation to jehad on the wall of a mosque in Faisalabad

One of the LeT men, Hafiz Saeed

Kiran and
Pooja Bhatt

Mahesh Bhatt holding baby Rahul as
U.G. Krishnamurti looks on

Pooja, Kiran, Rahul and
Mahesh Bhatt

Kiran, Rahul and
Mahesh Bhatt

Rahul Bhatt at the age of twelve

Rahul Bhatt with his bodyguard Carlos in Amsterdam

Just like me, David had a passion for books on military and warfare. He told me that he made it a point to read every night and worked on extending his vocabulary by learning a new word every day. He was very cosmopolitan in his ways and words.

I, on my part, love my action thrillers, my undercover heroes and my secret agents, and I enjoy my huge collection of books and movies based on these characters. Given the way he looked and sounded, it wasn't hard to think of David as an undercover agent. It was like watching a reel hero come alive.

During one of these meetings, David told me that he wanted to take Vilas and me to Pakistan. He referred to the Afghanistan-Pakistan border area as the wild wild west. But I was scared to go there, and told him so. I told him that I was afraid I would be kidnapped and murdered like Daniel Pearl. To this David said that nobody would dare to touch me if I was with him. He sounded very confident.

Then he said something that, at that time, I assumed was in jest.

'You know,' David said, 'all you guys have to do is change your names. People in that part of the world might not like Indians.' He waved his hand at Vilas. 'We can name Vilas here Akbar!'

We laughed at Vilas's incredulous face. The very thought of the hardcore Shiv Sainik being rechristened with a Muslim name was hilarious.

David then looked at me and said, 'Maybe you should have a name like Mohammed Atta!'

We laughed and dismissed the matter. David didn't bring it up again either.

Looking back, I feel a shiver run down my spine as I realize how devious David was.

THIRTEEN

By now, Behera had Headley all figured out. Yesterday, there had been a slip on his part, when he had inadvertently shown his surprise upon hearing Headley curse in flawless, unaccented Hindi. He had violated the first rule of a good interrogator—he had allowed himself to become vulnerable enough to be thrown off balance by a suspect's confession. And now he was afraid he had lost the advantage, the upper hand.

But as Headley walked in, his smile and swagger in place, Behera realized that it made no difference to Headley whether Behera felt he had slipped up or not. Headley was one of the most confident and self-assured criminals Behera had ever interrogated.

The muted tapping of the laptop's keys—his partner's—stopped as Headley drew back his chair and sat down, halfway between arrogance and cooperation.

'You were telling us about befriending Rahul and Vilas to try and target the Shiv Sena and Bollywood,' Behera said.

'I know exactly where I was, sir,' Headley replied, cocksure as ever, and started talking.

Before my recce of Delhi in September 2007, I had been concentrating fully on Mumbai. My friends in Pakistan—Sajid Mir, Major Iqbal and all my other Lashkar masters—were happy with my reconnaissance so far. They were also satisfied with my reportage and kept suggesting new places and new targets for me every time I visited Mumbai. I was only too happy to oblige.

I stayed in Mumbai from 20 March to 7 June 2007, leaving briefly in the middle, in May, to spend three days with my wife Shazia and my children in Dubai. My handlers were unaware of this short hiatus, although I kept Tahawwur Rana informed of my movements.

By the time I returned to Mumbai on 20 May—my fourth trip—I knew the city well. I had travelled the length and breadth of it, and I knew its layout like the back of my hand, especially South Mumbai. Most of the targets I had identified were in that part of the city.

I was sure that of the many potential targets, the Taj Mahal Hotel and the Trident Hotel were the most prominent and held the maximum promise as far as my plan was concerned. But I knew—I had also been told by my masters—that just these would not do. I had to scout for more targets.

I started casting my net a little wider, visiting various places across the city, including Sena Bhavan, which I was convinced had to be one of the targets. In fact, later on, in April 2008, we even decided to set our sights on the Bhabha Atomic Research Centre (BARC), which is India's premier multi-disciplinary nuclear research facility. It had never been targeted before, as the entire campus of BARC is well protected by mountains on one side and the sea on the other. But if Major Iqbal, Sajid and their plans were to be believed, and if I could conduct a good enough recce and manage to provide accurate details about the layout of BARC, perhaps it would not remain as impregnable this time as it had been in the past.

So I made several trips to Chembur to figure out how BARC could be attacked. I checked out the campus out from all sides, and even went up into the mountains that were adjacent to it; I secured a coign of vantage from where I could survey the area around BARC, and identify possible entry and exit routes. I left no stone unturned in my efforts, but try as I might, I could not find a way into the impregnable fortress-like nuclear facility. I told myself that there was always a way, and one only had to look hard enough to find it, and so I decided to come back later.

Sometimes, there would be strange instructions from my Pakistani handlers. For instance, in July 2008, I received one of the oddest instructions I'd got so far: to buy ten religious threads or wristbands from some Hindu temple. I had no idea why I was given this order as such wristbands are worn predominantly by Hindus and not by Muslims. But I had to carry out my orders to the letter. I also understood that I was supposed to know only as much as was essential and my masters would not tell me every detail of the operation they were planning.

So I went in search of the most famous temple in Mumbai, and in due course, I was directed to the Siddhivinayak Temple in Dadar. I decided to go to the temple with Vilas and Rahul. I called them up and told them that I wanted to visit the most famous temple in the city, and people had told me that it was the Siddhivinayak. When I asked them if they would accompany me, both Rahul and Vilas agreed.

We went to the temple on a Tuesday. I was amazed to see that even on a weekday there was a huge queue to get inside the temple. For some strange reason, Tuesday had been designated the day for the deity, Ganesha. I could not understand why God needed to be worshipped just on one particular day.

The queue snaked its way out from inside the temple and spilled onto the streets, and I saw the devotees waiting patiently for their turn. I was a little dismayed at this long queue, but I had my instructions. So I stood in the queue with the devotees, and so did Rahul and Vilas, and I could tell that they were surprised that I was not deterred by the long wait.

The three of us stood for several hours in that queue, until we finally got our turn and made our way inside. I bought the ten wristbands that I had been instructed to. Although Rahul was quite indifferent, Vilas was curious about why I, an American, wanted to buy wristbands, a symbol of the Hindu religion, and that too, not one but ten. I told him that they were for friends of mine who were interested in Hindu deities and worship.

It was then that I had an inkling of what my masters were probably planning. It suddenly struck me that at least ten men would come from Pakistan to India for some reason, and that these wristbands were for them so they could pass off as Hindus.

Behera instantly recalled that when Ajmal Kasab was captured by the Mumbai Police, he had been wearing a wristband. It had baffled the Mumbai cops for a long time—why would a Pakistani terrorist wear a wristband from a Hindu temple in Mumbai? Did they plan to mislead the cops? Or did they have far more nefarious designs? Behera remembered that Kasab was also carrying fake identity cards that made him out to be a student of a Bengaluru college.

Headley's voice jolted him back to the present.

Almost every day was spent scouting for places in the city that were vulnerable to attack. After all the spying and snooping around,

I needed an outlet or some kind of entertainment in the evenings to relax.

There was a bakery in Colaba, a very famous one, where, once in a while, a beautiful girl could be seen at the counter. She appeared to be in her mid-twenties, and whenever I went past the shop, she never failed to attract my attention. I decided to find out more about her, maybe develop a friendship with her, take her out to dinner. I hoped she would provide the distraction I needed after my work during the day.

Just to impress her, I would go to the bakery and buy pastries worth Rs 2,000 at a time. Slowly, I managed to catch the girl's attention, and it turned out that my purchases had made her think that I was an affluent American businessman. Soon, she started to give me her full attention. She would take me around the shop and chat with me as I selected pastries. And so we became friends.

The girl was half my age, but she was very intelligent and extremely articulate. I realized that she was fantastic company. I met her a couple of times, but never summoned up enough courage to ask her to bed.

After we had been out with each other a few times, her mannerism and demeanour told me that she was getting serious about me. This was confirmed just a few days later when she took me to meet her father at her home. He turned out to be a nice man, and he behaved very warmly with me and was very hospitable. He clearly loved his daughter, and I could tell that he was unhappy that she had brought home someone who was twice her age. He kept trying to gauge how serious I was about her, and whether I was good enough for her. Nothing came of this, though, although I kept in touch with my beautiful friend for a long time.

Somehow women have been my weakness—a fact I had grown to acknowledge. During the time I was dating the girl from the bakery, I happened to bump into a Bollywood starlet while I was working out at Moksh. She was very attractive, and I liked her very much. I remember watching her in a Bollywood flick where she plays an authority on the Mumbai underworld. I liked the way she portrayed her character in the movie.

Whenever I found this starlet working out at the gym, my eyes would stray towards her; I shamelessly lusted after her. I would often stop during my workout session and admire her flawless figure that sported all the right curves in the right places.

Even as I was dreaming about these two women, another actress who was rising fast in Bollywood caught my attention. She was beautiful and curvaceous, and I even contemplated paying to go on the sets of one of her shoots and meeting her. But I was told that her English was not very good, and I was not willing to expose my knowledge of Hindi to her. So I kept admiring her from a distance, and decided that someday later I would use Rahul to get to her, meet her over a cup of coffee or dinner and speak to her in broken Hindi, as if I had picked it up while I was in Mumbai.

Such were the evenings that I spent, either on dates or in silent contemplation of feminine beauty and the desires it stirred.

It was during that same trip in July 2008 that another message came to me through Tahawwur Rana from my Pakistani handlers. I was told to make a trip to Pune.

When I told Rahul that I would be going to Pune, he was excited and wanted to tag along; he had a girlfriend in Pune and had good reason to accompany me. Vilas too wanted to come. But I couldn't have that. If they came with me, they would definitely smell a rat, which I couldn't afford at all. So I told them that I would have to go to Pune on my own as I had a lot of work there. I also told them I was thinking of setting up another branch of First World Immigration. It would require considerable time and a lot of effort on my part, which would leave me with little opportunity to spend time with them. Both Rahul and Vilas accepted my explanation.

My brief was to visit all the places where westerners and white people tended to congregate in large numbers. The idea was to create international furore about the attack, by making sure that there were large numbers of foreign casualties. Indians had been killed before, and it lacked novelty. There had been so many blasts and attacks where Indians were targeted, but they had never had a serious impact. So now, my LeT and ISI bosses wanted to target places in India that were frequented by foreigners. This was also one of the reasons why I had chosen south Mumbai as a potential target. The concentration of foreigners there is far higher than in any other part of the city. If many foreigners were killed, it would grab the attention of the international community, it would shock everyone, and we would get the respect we deserved.

The primary target that my handlers were eyeing, and for which I had been sent to scout out the area, was the Osho ashram in Pune. There would be a few Indians at the ashram, but most of Rajneesh's followers were either Europeans or Americans. So any kind of blast at the ashram would create a huge clamour internationally.

I did a thorough recce of the ashram and realized that the place was virtually a fortress, made so by the workers of the ashram themselves. It would be difficult to penetrate it or attack it from anywhere at all. Unlike the places in Mumbai that were proving to be a cakewalk, the entry points to the ashram were all guarded fiercely and there were several rounds of registration to complete, preventing anyone from simply walking in. Security guards crawled all over the place. The receptionist too was a very inquisitive person, and took down all kinds of details before allowing anyone inside.

So now I had to come up with a viable alternative target. I spent a long time scouring the areas around the ashram, and finally hit upon a place which was frequented by foreigners and was also visited by those at the ashram. It was the famous German Bakery.

The bakery was very close to the ashram, almost diagonally opposite the Jewish Chabad House. During the evening hours, foreigners made a beeline to the bakery to buy freshly baked bread and other products. I did some quick calculations and realized that if planned properly, a big enough explosion at the bakery would affect the ashram itself and draw the attention of the international community.

I also visited several military installations in Pune, looking for a possible attack site. Unfortunately, I could not find any loopholes in the security there. I drew my conclusions from the recces, prepared my report, and returned to Mumbai.

By the time the July 2008 trip drew to an end, my targets were slowly becoming clearer. I had decided that south Mumbai would be the main target, and that the German Bakery in Pune could also be one. We were still to figure out whether an attack on BARC would be viable or not, even though I was very keen on it.

Behera interrupted. 'Mr Headley, you told us about your visiting several military installations. What about the attack on the CRPF camp in Rampur?'

Headley looked puzzled. 'What do you mean? When was this attack?'

'In January 2008.'

'I'm afraid I have no information about it.' Headley paused, and seemed to think. Then he said, 'I know that sometime in January 2008 Zaki-ur-Rehman Lakhvi had met a couple of LeT operatives who had escaped from India. But that is all I know.'

Behera sat back in his chair, nodding. His assumption was correct. The LeT were working on a need-to-know basis, and nobody was given the entire picture. Even someone like

Headley didn't know all that was going on. Behera gestured to Headley to carry on.

The Sena Bhavan was among these high-profile targets—it had been on my mind from the very start. I believed I had already made inroads there, since I had been cultivating Vilas's friendship for quite some time; in fact, by July 2008, we had been great friends for about a year. The previous year, I had done enough to ensure that he valued me and my friendship highly. In May 2007, I had even organized a birthday party for him. I knew this would endear him to me even further, and he would trust me completely.

Vilas was crossing forty, and had once told me that he had never been given a party for his birthday, coming as he did from a lower-middle-class background. No one had ever cut a cake for him or lit candles or even wished him a happy birthday, for that matter. It was rather sad, and I knew instantly that the best gesture I could make was to organize a birthday party for him. We had the party on 30 May at a south Mumbai joint.

When Vilas saw what I had done, he was speechless. I couldn't count the number of times he thanked me. Throughout the party, too, he remained extremely emotional, visibly overwhelmed by the attention he was getting from all the people who had come to the party. I found that Rahul too was delighted that I had done something like this for his friend. The party served another purpose—it brought me closer to Rahul Bhatt.

In fact, I consider this party that I threw for Vilas to be the smartest thing I did on that particular trip. At an expense of a few thousand rupees and a couple of hours, I had managed to turn Vilas into a steadfast ally and a friend for life.

FOURTEEN

Life holds many secrets and the unravelling of these is one of its greatest joys. But I will never be able to fathom certain secrets, for instance, the ones inside David Headley's mind; what he thought and how he functioned the way he did remain a mystery to me. This man came out of nowhere and became such a good friend that not a day went by when I did not speak to him or think about him or SMS him.

David had many endearing qualities that charmed everyone who came in contact with him. I am not friendly and gregarious by nature. Having grown up the way I did, it is hardly surprising that I am a bit of a recluse. But David made me open up to him in a way that I never could have imagined. While I remained aloof and isolated from people around me, I loved talking to him. He often came down to my place in Bandra, and we would sit out on the terrace and watch the city go by, talking for hours on end. It was difficult not to talk to him when he was with you, and it was impossible to say no to him.

Yet, there were times when we would both lapse into a very comfortable, companionable silence during which we didn't speak a word to each other. David kind of grew on me; I felt comfortable with him.

Every time I looked at him, I felt happy that he was with me, and at the same time a little sad and wistful that my own father, Mr Mahesh Bhatt, was so unlike him. I started looking for Mr Bhatt in someone who came from across continents and over thousands of miles, and was not even an Indian. If only my father had been as friendly, as warm and helpful as this guy.

What made it such a pleasure talking to him was that David always made it a point to talk about things I liked and was interested in. I would ask him all kinds of questions and he would have answers for each of them. Right from the beginning of our association, he knew that I found security, crime and related subjects most interesting. I always looked forward to his responses to questions I had on these subjects. Once, in 2007, I had sent him an email saying that I was researching the role of a suicide bomber as I was likely to land a role in a movie where I would be playing such a character. I asked him if he could suggest a couple of books that I might read to get into character.

He instantly replied to my mail with a few names: *The Kaoboys of Raw* by B. Raman, *Counterinsurgency* by David Kilcullen, *Killing Zone: A Professional's Guide to Preparing and Preventing Ambushes* by Gary Stubblefield and Mark Monday. He even told me that he would get them for me from the US the next time he came to Mumbai. In the same email, he told me that he had ordered a few books for himself—*International Fugitives, Boxing Mastery, Ragner's Guide to Interviews, Investigations, and Interrogations,* and *The Brutal Art of Ripping and Poking.* I knew that he was interested in all these subjects, so much so that he wanted his son to grow up to be a commando.

David was always very supportive of me, a fact I realized during one of our conversations. It was sometime in late 2007, and we were sitting in my terrace garden and chatting. The conversation turned to movies and then to my own family and the film industry. I had once told him that my father had long ago promised a launch pad for me in Bollywood. Suddenly, David turned to me and said, 'What's taking your father so long? Why isn't he helping you?'

I didn't know how to respond as I myself didn't have an answer to that question; in fact, I still haven't found the answer. So I kept quiet.

David was quick to sense my mood and asked me, 'Rahul, how much does it cost to make a movie?'

'Oh, around five to seven crore rupees for a small budget film,' I told him.

He seemed a bit nonplussed, and said, 'Okay, how much is that in dollars?'

I did some mental arithmetic and replied, 'Roughly two million dollars.'

He said, 'Hey! That's not a problem at all! I'll speak to my partner and see if we can raise the money for your film!'

I couldn't believe my ears. I knew that he was genuinely concerned about me, and also that he liked the idea of being part of the glitz and glamour of Bollywood. He used to refer to me as his favourite hero, and we had often talked, though not seriously, about making an Indian version of *The Godfather*, in which Vilas would play the role of Luca Brasi. But this was unexpected.

'Are you kidding?' I asked incredulously.

David laughed and said, 'Sure! Why not? Let me see what I can do, okay?'

I was speechless. I had no reason to doubt his concern and his interest in launching me in a film. All I could see was a friend, a father figure, helping me realize my dream.

It is true that Vilas is the one who introduced me to David, but ultimately, I became closer to him. Vilas was David's gymnasium trainer, but I was more of a surrogate son to him, if there is such a term.

In fact, David began trusting me so much that he started taking steroid cycles from me. I injected him several times with IGF-2 and charged him 800 dollars for the entire cycle, which he happily paid.

David and I travelled all over town in those days. We went to Ayub's and Bade Miyan in Colaba, where we would gorge on delicious chicken. He came across as someone immensely interested in everything about Mumbai, which made him a delightful companion, for I love the city too. And he was always taking pictures and recording videos. I remember being pleasantly surprised at his genuine enthusiasm to arm and shoot that camera of his.

Once, during one of our frequent trips out, we went to Big Cinemas Metro, which is located near Azad Maidan and the Mumbai Police's Special Branch, to watch a movie. The show was supposed to start at 3 p.m., but we had arrived half an hour early. I excused myself for a while and left him standing alone at the entrance of the theatre to go to an ATM. A strange sight greeted me when I came back. David had spotted a Bohra priest, complete with a flowing beard, and was talking to him earnestly. As I approached, I heard the conversation between the two, and I realized that he had got into a very random argument with the gentleman.

I watched spellbound as the two of them stood there engaged in earnest debate for at least twenty to twenty-five minutes in front of all the people who had come to watch the movie. In fact, some people were even listening to the argument. I could not figure out why David had to accost the unsuspecting old man, who most certainly had no idea of what was coming when this huge, tall American had walked up to him and started arguing about the real meaning of Islam and why he believed in it and so on. The poor man had to defend Islam in the face of this sudden onslaught, and I found it a hilarious, if somewhat bizarre, spectacle. Finally, I had to intervene and tell David to leave the poor guy alone, and dragged him in to watch the movie.

Meanwhile, one day Vilas told us that he had set up a meeting with the Shiv Sena for David. David had been telling Vilas that he wanted to know everything about the Sena, and that he was keen on getting an audience with Sena supremo Bal Thackeray. Vilas had already taken him to the Shiv Sena Bhavan in Dadar. David had been enthralled and had taken a number of photographs. Vilas said that he would take David to meet Thackeray the following week at Matoshree, the politician's residence in Bandra East.

David was very excited at this opportunity and egged Vilas on to tell us more about the Sena. While Vilas was elaborating on the meeting, the party and his leader's charisma, David suddenly turned to me and said, 'Rahul, do you know there are 241 Sena shakhas in Mumbai?'

I was taken aback. I was a bona fide resident of Mumbai and Vilas was a Shiv Sena worker. But neither of us was aware of such a fact. And here was this American, a foreigner, standing in front of us and spouting details about Mumbai, including a minor statistic that we should have known!

I asked him how he was aware of such specifics. His answer stunned both Vilas and me. 'You know, guys,' he said, 'according to the US Department of State, the Shiv Sena is a terrorist organization. So the US has all kinds of data.' Vilas and I looked at each other and I knew that he shared my awe.

It was decided that sometime in the next couple of days, Vilas would pick David up from his hotel in south Mumbai and they would go to Bandra together.

Vilas later told me that David seemed quite excited when they arrived at their destination and told the men there that they had come to meet Bal Thackeray. They were then directed to a man named Rajaram Rege, who was probably the secretary to Mr Thackeray as well as to his son Uddhav.

But David was out of luck that day. Rege told them that Thackeray was too busy with several high-profile meetings and would not be able to meet them. He apologized to them and told them to give him details about why they wanted to meet him and said that he would set up a meeting very soon.

Vilas told me that within minutes, David had charmed the man with his vast knowledge of Mumbai and the Shiv Sena. Rege was practically eating out of David's hand as he took down all the details, including addresses and phone numbers, and promised them as they left that a meeting with Thackeray would be set up for sometime next week.

As soon as the two of them came out of the building, David stopped and said that he wanted to take a few photographs of Matoshree. Vilas was amused as he watched David rush about taking pictures from different angles. He was using his digital camera, with which one can shoot both stills and video. Of course, Vilas had no way of knowing whether David was shooting stills or recording.

For nearly fifteen minutes, David kept clicking away on his camera, saying that it was a historic place and that he had a lot of respect for Bal Thackeray, who he said was very famous and known to many people in America. Happy at his party supremo receiving such praise, Vilas humoured him and let him take as many pictures and record for as long as he wanted to.

Sometime later, when the three of us met again, I commented on the security at Bal Thackeray's residence, which was provided by his own party workers and by the State Reserve Police Force and various other security outfits. I remarked that Thackeray was definitely one of the best protected men in all of Asia, and that he had Z+ security.

David's reply was both shocking and impressive. He turned to me and said, 'You know what? There are many loopholes in that security setup. If you look carefully, you'll see that Thackeray is actually a sitting duck.'

I looked at David, wondering if he had really said that. He saw my quizzical expression and continued, 'Rahul, take it from me. A small bunch of desperadoes could break that security cover wide open and reach Thackeray. I have no idea why the police are so proud of the protection that he has been given. I can quite clearly see that he is not well protected at all.'

When we asked him how he knew of the loopholes for sure and what dangers he could see, David refused to elaborate.

Vilas and I looked at each other, puzzled. This man had been there for hardly a few minutes and had managed to assess the security of the area and had supposedly found several loopholes in it. And to top it all, he was saying that Thackeray could be assassinated at will! David never ceased to amaze me, and I told him that. My conviction that he really was an American agent grew even stronger.

David seemed to be in a mood to talk that day. He said there were many things that the Mumbai Police didn't know or were clueless about. He also said that Indian security agencies were not aware of a host of important things, and that there were thousands of small things that the average smart spy could take advantage of.

Surprised, I asked him what these things were.

I half expected David to fall silent, as he usually did when any of us broached such a subject. But that day, he just kept talking.

'Let me give you an example,' he said. 'You see these mobile phones that we carry? They are all connected to the service provider's signal tower. Now, suppose I don't want my movements to be traced via this phone. Well, it can be done very easily. Let's say I wanted to meet you in Worli. I would come to Lalbagh, and this would be traced by the mobile towers. The moment I reach Lalbagh, all I have to do is switch off my phone. Now there is no trace on me, and no one can know where I am. So, from Lalbagh I can travel to Worli, and from there I can come back to Bandra without being traced. Back at Bandra, when I switch my mobile phone on, the agencies will immediately deduce that I left Lalbagh and arrived in Bandra, but they would have no idea of what happened in between. What I did and where I went would remain completely untraceable.'

I was amazed, but also wondered out loud if there were any agencies that were capable of tracing a suspect who tried to shake off a shadow by such methods. David replied, 'Well, it's only the FBI which can ensure that a dead or switched-off phone in your pocket becomes a microphone that can relay each and every piece of information to the listeners without any hindrance. Not many others can.'

He then said that switching off one's mobile phone was actually a very basic and simple trick, but there were many such tricks with which spies could easily mislead anyone tracking them. He laughed at the Indian agencies, who, he said, thought they knew everything and believed that the situation was under control and any such subversive designs could easily be tracked.

This convinced me beyond all doubt that David was anything but a businessman, and that his being an immigration lawyer was just a front. I was sure he was some kind of agent for a security or intelligence agency, given the knowledge that he displayed.

Another incident around this time gave me a glimpse of David's chameleon-like ability to slip into any role instantly. I had sold a Cybex treadmill to my uncle Mukesh Bhatt for Rs 1.35 lakh. My aunt wanted to use one and my uncle didn't like to go out to exercise either, preferring to walk for sixty minutes on a treadmill at home instead. Since I had some contacts at Cybex, I ensured that the machine was delivered with utmost care to my uncle's residence in Bandra.

Unfortunately, within a few weeks, the treadmill developed a technical snag and was rendered almost unusable. Mukesh and his wife Nilima kept calling me and asking me to come and see if I could identify what the problem was and if I could do anything about it.

One day, when I was sitting in a cafe in Bandra with David, chatting about inconsequential things, I received one such call from my uncle. He reminded me that he had paid a lot of money and didn't want to see the machine go to waste. Since I was close to their house, I decided I would drop in and see what I could do. I asked David if he would mind tagging along with me for just a bit, to which he answered that he would be delighted.

We went to Mukesh Bhatt's place, which was within walking distance from the cafe. When we reached, my uncle wasn't at home, it was my aunt who welcomed us. She gazed curiously at David, who cut a rather impressive figure in his green polo-neck T-shirt and jeans, with his differently coloured eyes and ponytail.

On the spur of the moment, I decided to play a prank on both David and my aunt. When she looked at David, expecting me to introduce them, I walked up to her and said, 'You guys were so upset and distressed about the treadmill that I spoke to the people at Cybex. This gentleman here is David Headley, the vice-president of Cybex India, who has come personally at my request to see if he can help you.'

My aunt looked at David, clearly impressed that the vice-president himself had come to look at the faulty machine. I waited to see how David would react, and was mentally already chuckling, imagining him fumble with the situation.

But I shouldn't have bothered trying to trick David. Once again, he amazed me with his presence of mind and his chameleon-like personality.

David slipped into the role of vice-president, Cybex India, with élan. 'Don't worry, Mrs Bhatt. If you are so dissatisfied with the product, I shall personally see to it that your machine is replaced completely free of charge. You needn't worry about the machine at all, and I apologize that you have been so inconvenienced. We want our customers to be 100 per cent satisfied. They should have no cause for complaint at all,' David rattled off, sounding thoroughly reassuring and convincing. I had expected him to fumble, or stay quiet and just nod, and was floored at how he rose to the occasion.

We came out of the house laughing at the prank. That day I discovered an entirely new side to David, a mischievous streak I had never seen in him before. I realized once again that the man could change roles and step into the shoes of any man that he wanted to in a matter of seconds, and do so convincingly.

Once, I suggested to David that he and I launch an executive protection agency in Mumbai, as I was also interested in crime and security and he was a storehouse of information on the subject. Initially, David was not very keen, but after I explained my idea to him at some length, he seemed to fall in with it and said that he would speak to some friends of his in the US who were in the same business and see if such a venture was possible and whether it would be profitable or not. However, we never got around to taking the idea any further.

Throughout the early part of 2008, David and I kept meeting each other on and off. Vilas told me a very strange thing one day, which I did not understand at the time. In hindsight, though, it becomes clear. Vilas said that once, when he had gone to pick David up from where he was staying, he had seen the American reading a book in Arabic. At the time I dismissed it without a thought, saying David was probably just skimming through a volume which he didn't understand but was curious about. I thought that maybe it was some kind of religious text.

Now I know why he had that book on him, why an American would carry an Arabic book with him.

As the world has discovered, in his head David wasn't an American at all.

FIFTEEN

'May I have some coffee please?'

Headley's request was immediately fulfilled; the FBI man signalled to the camera, and in less than a minute, a steaming cup of coffee arrived.

Behera was impatient to get on with the interrogation. He said, 'So what happened next?'

Headley took a sip of coffee, leaned back and closed his eyes. Then he started to speak.

By the time I arrived in Mumbai on 10 April 2008, my seventh visit, I had been to all the important locations in Mumbai that I thought could be targeted. All the sites—which included the Chhatrapati Shivaji Terminus (CST), known till recently as the Victoria Terminus (VT), the Taj Mahal Hotel near the Gateway of India, the Leopold Cafe near the Taj, and the Trident Hotel—had been identified. I felt these were important as they were all famous landmarks of the city and were almost always crowded. The casualties would be huge. And it would create a major furore internationally.

But my surveillance was not complete. I had not yet filmed or videographed any of the targets. This was essential, as it would help the strategists planning the attack to visualize the area and prepare accordingly. My Pakistani handlers had confirmed that I would have to make videos of the targets. And they would have to be detailed enough for the attackers, who would not be locals or even Indians, to be able to identify everything around them at first glance and know exactly what to do without getting lost or disoriented.

Major Iqbal gave me a camera and taught me the finer points of video recording. He first showed me how people usually shoot videos using a digital camera, and then demonstrated how to do it from a different perspective. He taught me how to record a target from a terrorist's point of view. For instance, the height of a building is very important, and so is the floor on which the attack is to be carried out. Everything in between can be covered if, say, you manage to plant a bomb in the foundations of the building. You can find your way out and then detonate the explosive from afar, without any risk to yourself. However, the situation is very different if the plan is to launch a full-fledged attack.

When targeting a tall building, it is important to know the height of the structure. If you manage to sneak into the building and reach the top floor, you will have to know how to escape from it too— either by jumping on to a neighbouring building or by climbing down somehow.

These were the things—the minute details—that Major Iqbal taught me to notice and capture on film. When I went back to India, I used his technique and recorded all the targets I had identified as well as the surrounding areas very carefully, taking care not to leave out any detail. To the world, I looked like any interested tourist taking pictures and recording videos. But I managed to capture everything on film—every entry and exit point, each fire exit, the security, the guard shifts, the local populace. I left nothing out, from the Taj Mahal Hotel to CST.

I even went to the Sena Bhavan a second time to conduct a video surveillance. I chanced upon the Shiv Sena PRO Rajaram Rege, who remembered me from our first meeting at Matoshree. We spoke for a while, and I took him out to lunch. I must have made an impression on the man, because he emailed me several times afterwards.

Rege's emails were full of self-promotion and the promise of big bucks if we set up business in Mumbai. He kept telling me that he had a lot of powerful political connections, both in the Indian government and the Maharashtra government, and that he was handling projects worth hundreds of crores. He was eager to be the middleman if I could bring some major US companies to invest in India. He even told me that there would be some under-the-table dealings which would be profitable for both him and me. He apparently expected a donation from the US to the tune of ten lakh USD. He also kept asking me if he could find opportunities for himself in the US, and claimed that he had sixteen years of experience in the IT sector.

I checked with my superiors about how to handle the man, given that he was a part of the Shiv Sena. Major Iqbal asked me how I could use him to my advantage, and finally gave me carte blanche to handle him as I saw fit.

I replied to Rege saying that I was quite interested in doing business with him, although I didn't go into specifics. I also told him to provide me with some details of the finances he was in charge of. We exchanged a couple of emails, but nothing came of them.

The videography continued into my eighth visit to Mumbai, in July 2008. It was then that I found another target. As I moved around Colaba, taking in the sights around the Taj and Leopold Cafe, I chanced upon a Jewish centre, off the Colaba Causeway from where one approaches the Taj. It was a five-storey building called Nariman House. I asked around as surreptitiously as I could, and found out that the building was actually a Chabad Lubavitch Jewish religious centre, also known as the Mumbai Chabad House. It was described as the epicentre of the Jewish community in the city.

When I told Sajid Mir and Major Iqbal about Nariman House, they rubbished my words, saying that it wasn't just a Chabad house, and that it was actually a front for the Mossad. But they were wrong. When I visited Nariman House, I spoke to the people there and realized that it was a religious centre, and nothing to do with the Mossad.

At Chabad House, I met the man who ran the place, Rabbi Gavriel Holtzberg, and his wife Rivkah. To make sure that I didn't do anything to give away my identity, I had procured a book titled *To Pray As a Jew*. I had studied it thoroughly before I ventured into Holtzberg's territory, and I realized that the Muslim way of offering namaz and the way the Jewish prayed were very similar. Both genuflect, both prostrate, and except for the specific words they recite, the actions are more or less similar. So it was very easy for me to imitate their prayers and pass myself off as a Jew without raising any suspicion.

I stayed at Chabad House for a day and interacted with everyone, including the rabbi. I did not notice any signs of Mossad activity. Since I had been well trained, I knew what to look for. If I couldn't find anything, it meant that my handlers were wrong. However, I agreed with Lashkar's basic principle—that Jews had to be eradicated from the face of the earth—and I decided that a bomb should definitely be planted at Nariman House and it should most certainly be one of the target sites.

My handlers liked my findings and my idea that Nariman House and its rabbi and his family should be a target. However, they didn't confirm anything.

Earlier, in September 2007, I had convinced Vilas to take me to the golf course of the Willingdon Sports Club to see if I could get a membership. I had learned to play golf in Lahore and had even bought a golf kit. I knew that an attack on a posh high-society golf club in Mumbai would be the icing on the cake. However, the club had very strict rules about membership and I couldn't get in. Since I had little use for my golf kit, I gave it to Vilas before leaving India that time. Almost a year later, armed with a camera, I recorded the layout of the club in detail.

In the guise of an affluent businessman on a work trip to Mumbai, or as a tourist, I managed to sneak into all the corridors and nooks and crannies of the Taj, which is an old Gothic structure, and realized that the old building of the Taj was connected to its new building. During my reconnaissance of the hotel, I even recorded the interior of Jazdar, the jewellery shop inside. Nobody suspected a thing. I walked around the entire perimeter of CST, from the old terminus to the new one, recording every minute detail. I even got some videos of the Mumbai Central railway station, another busy spot. Nobody would get lost if they memorized the details captured on these videos. My work was appreciated by my handlers too; they especially liked my video of Chabad House.

In April 2008, I identified and filmed one of the most important sites: a safe and secure landing spot for the attackers who would arrive in Mumbai.

The assignment was slightly tricky. There was no way that the attackers could enter via the land route, and air travel was, of course, out of the question. The Lashkar strategists had worked their way around this problem. Karachi has a geographical proximity to the Mumbai Harbour via the Arabian Sea, and so the attackers, I was told, would come from the sea.

My handlers and several others met in Muzaffarabad to discuss this matter. The meeting was held at Zaki's place. Initially, Sajid didn't show much interest in taking me to the meeting, but at the last minute, he changed his mind and asked me to accompany him. Apart from the two of us, the others who were present at the meeting were Zaki, Muzammil and Abu Kahafa. Also at the meeting was a clean-shaven man with a crew cut, who appeared to be in his mid-thirties. Remember the frogman I told you about, the one I had met in Muzaffarabad? It was the same man—Abdur Rehman. I was introduced to him as Abdul Qadir. His manners and the way he held himself showed that he was from the Pakistan Navy.

Zaki wanted to figure out the transportation and landing of the attackers with the help of the frogman. They discussed various landing options along the coast of Mumbai, using a sea chart the frogman had brought with him. A plan was floated: the attackers would be dropped off at some place around sixty or seventy kilometres from Mumbai city in order to avoid detection. But the frogman vetoed this plan, saying that the sea would become rough after June.

On the second day, Rehman told me to check the position of Indian naval vessels in the Arabian Sea to avoid the possibility of a gunfight before the attackers even entered Indian waters. I said I would find out as much as I could. That was the last time I saw the frogman.

I came back to Mumbai on 10 April 2008, armed with instructions to find an entry point, and also to conduct a recce of BARC, which I've mentioned before. Apart from my trusty camera, my handlers had given me another piece of equipment to help aid my assignment—a Garmin GPS instrument. All I had to do was enter the coordinates of all the possible landing sites as well as the exact location of the targets, and it would acquaint my LeT masters with the layout of the city and help them figure out the best place to land in Mumbai.

Armed with these two gadgets, I set about my assignment. After having completed the BARC recce, I came back to south Mumbai, hired a boat at the Gateway of India, and started cruising along the Mumbai Harbour.

Very soon, I was openly filming along the coastline, expecting to be intercepted at some point by either the coastguard or the navy, especially since there was a naval base very close to the Taj. But to my amazement, I was not stopped even once, anywhere, by anyone. I managed to move around unhindered and undetected, without a single restriction or question. The men who handled the boat kept quiet too, as I had not bargained with them over the cost of hiring it out. They were glad to assist me with whatever I wanted.

From the Gateway of India, I carried out video surveillance of all the places that would be attacked, but somehow, I could not locate one place that would be perfect as a landing spot for the attackers. As usual, according to our arrangement, I called Rana and informed him about my mission and all that I had done. But before signing off, I told him that I was not very happy with the video recording and told him that I needed a little more time to identify a suitable landing site. Rana concurred with my decision to carry out further surveillance.

The next day, I went recording again, but this time from the Trident Hotel end of the city. Again, I moved around with my camera and took pictures and recorded everything without being stopped or questioned even once. The assignment was turning out to be easy, but I was still not happy.

I made another trip by boat in the vicinity of the Taj. That day it so happened that I landed up near Budhwar Park at Cuffe Parade. It wasn't thronging with people like the other beaches along the Mumbai coastline, and once the sun set, the place was quite dark. I realized that if the attackers came by night, they would have the perfect cover—the darkness of mother nature. Throughout my recce, I kept updating and loading the GPS device with all the coordinates.

I made one final boat trip into the waters of the Arabian Sea, this time from the Worli side. I took the boat all the way from Haji Ali, the famous mosque in the middle of the sea, to the Taj at the Gateway. By now I was quite used to not being intercepted. My activities, which could clearly be deemed very suspicious, went completely unnoticed—surprising, since Mumbai is supposed to be constantly on the radar of terrorists.

In between these trips, I also indulged in a little fishing to calm my mind. That too went unquestioned, even though I knew that I cut a strange spectacle, a white man on a local boat, catching fish with the local fishermen. I caught a decent number of fish, and gave them to Mrs Kripalani, the owner of Outram Hotel where I was staying.

I finally settled upon the Cuffe Parade area as the most promising landing spot. I was pleased with my work, and felt sorry for the complacent and self-important, pompous Indians for their 'oh, we are so secure' attitude. They would soon discover the perils of overconfidence and arrogance.

I called Rana and informed him that I had completed my assignment and found a good landing spot.

During my next visit to India in July 2008, I continued recording the targets, getting as much information as I could. I had done everything that the LeT and the ISI had asked me to do. By the end of July 2008, I had quite a substantial amount of recorded material. I was quite proud of my videos and knew that any attacker relying on these films would have no problem in finding their way around these landmarks.

In August 2008, when I went back to Pakistan, I faithfully reported to my bosses all the work I had done and the conclusions I had drawn. I had played my part in the scheme of things, and all that was required now was for them to identify the men who would attack Mumbai. I heard on the grapevine that ten men were already being trained for the attack, and wished them well.

When I met Sajid and Zaki, I learned that they had finally gone ahead with my recommendation and designated Chabad House as a target. Several other sites were also discussed as potential targets—Taj Presidency, World Trade Centre, Naval Air Station, Siddhivinayak Temple, the Maharashtra Police headquarters, the Mantralaya, the El Al Airlines office, the Bombay Stock Exchange and the Radio Club, among others. Zaki and Sajid had already discussed the options for the landing site and that too had been finalized.

I was most satisfied that they had chosen Chabad House as a target. I suppose Sajid had a hand in this; after all, he was a Saudi Salafi and he believed that Jews should be the number one target. And he was not the only one. When I had told Pasha about it, he too had liked the idea. It was at his insistence that I had recommended that Nariman House also be designated as a target.

Another point we discussed at that meeting was the egress of the attackers once the operation had been executed. The consensus was that the attackers would take a train or a bus bound for some place in north India, make their way to Kashmir, and take refuge there. Later, when I met Major Iqbal, he too emphasized the egress option for the attackers. We discussed the VT train schedules and the bus timings to figure out an escape route. Sajid even told me that he had dropped a couple of boys who were being trained because if the number of attackers became unwieldy, it would make an undetected escape to Kashmir that much more difficult.

However, the more we discussed it, the more the egress option appeared difficult. So we thought of establishing a stronghold somewhere, as an alternative. This slowly took precedence over the egress option. I believe the LeT, in keeping with the decision, started giving lectures to the attackers on Fazail-e-Shaheed and Fazail-e-Jehad (the merits of martyrdom and the excellence of jehad).

The next day, Abu Kahafa joined the meeting. We talked of the jewellery shop at the Taj. There was a plan to loot the shop and use the jewellery to raise funds, although I don't know how serious they were about actually doing it.

Meanwhile, Sajid and Zaki had come up with a Plan B, and prepared two sets of targets depending on the time of landing. Should they reach during the day, the Mumbai Police headquarters would be their first target. I must say I was impressed by the level of detail that went into planning the attack.

After a few days, I found out that Sajid had been shifted to Muridke, and so had the attackers. During this period, Hafiz Saeed, along with others like Bhutti, Nasar Javed and Abdur Rehman Maki, made regular trips to Muridke and helped in training and motivating the boys. I also found out that an Indian, probably from Maharashtra, who was considered an asset, was finally dropped as Sajid wanted to use him elsewhere. I don't know what became of this Indian boy, but I'm pretty sure he wasn't part of the group that attacked Mumbai.

Sometime in August 2008, Sajid gave me one last assignment. He told me to go to the Wagah border, which is a thirty-minute drive from Lahore, to check the cell phone connectivity of one of the SIM cards which the attackers would use in Mumbai. It was an Indian SIM card of the Vodafone company.

In September 2008, on the instructions of my Lashkar masters, I returned one last time before the attack to Mumbai, to give finishing touches to my reconnaissance, to tie up any and all loose ends, and conduct final, last-minute checks of the targets. When I returned to Pakistan, my handlers congratulated me on my work and told me that my job was done.

I had performed my role to their expectations. Sajid and Zaki told me not to bother about the operation any more, and advised me to lie low for a while. For safety's sake, I shifted my family—my wife Shazia and my four children—to the US on 8 September 2008. Tahawwur Rana's family received them in Chicago.

My handlers also told me that my larger mission was far from over. I would have to go back to India and carry out reconnaissance of other Jewish centres across the country. I happily agreed.

Meanwhile, there were a few personal upheavals in my life. Faiza Outalha, my other wife, met Hafiz Saeed in early September. Earlier, too, she had met senior officials in the police and created problems for me. In fact, I was even taken into custody by the Lahore Police on her complaint, and had to spend eight days in the Race Course police station before my father-in-law (Shazia's father) bailed me out. Major Iqbal also helped to procure my release. Hafiz Saeed then wanted me to reconcile with Faiza, but I told him that it would be difficult as I was busy with the LeT's operational activities. He understood my compulsions.

There were a couple of hiccups with the Mumbai attack mission as well. The first attempt in September 2008 during Ramzan had to be aborted. Everything had been readied for the attack, but the boat that had been bought for the travel to Mumbai from Karachi, with five lakh rupees that were provided by Major Iqbal, hit a rock and had to be junked. The attackers were safe, as they had all been wearing life jackets, which had been procured at my insistence. Major Iqbal assured all of us that it wouldn't happen again, and that the next boat was ready, with weapons, ammunition and equipment. He told us that the government would clear it. Hafiz Saeed too had given his full approval for the attack. In fact, he was abreast of each and every stage of planning. Sajid Mir too confirmed this.

The plan received another setback in the second half of October. I was in Karachi in November 2008, and met Sajid at a MacDonald's outlet. He told me that the second attempt to capture an Indian boat had failed. When they approached the boat, the Indian crew aboard had become suspicious and steered it away. There was an exchange of gunfire, but the boat got away.

I knew how important the attack on Mumbai was to the LeT and the ISI. In December 2007, I had received instructions from Sajid to meet him—in Rawalpindi this time, instead of Muzaffarabad. I reached 'Pindi on 27 December 2007, the day Benazir Bhutto was assassinated. Abu Hamza came on a motorcycle to pick me up from the bus stand at 'Pindi. Soon, word of the attack on Benazir reached us, and we all assembled at a Lashkar safe house near Ayub Colony. We talked about the assassination attempt, and how it would affect the future of Pakistan. I recollect that all those present at the safe house, including Abu Hamza and Sajid, were praying that Benazir should not survive the attempt. But even then, the most important thing on everyone's mind was the Mumbai attack. Despite the events of the day, we still had serious discussions about it and about the Taj Hotel in Colaba.

In fact, the plan to attack Mumbai had not been formed overnight. It had developed from a split in ideology, the main issue being, whether the focus should be on the jehad in Kashmir or Afghanistan. People like Abdur Rehman and Pasha had already split from the LeT. They were more interested in carrying on the jehad in Afghanistan than in Kashmir. Zaki had a serious problem holding the LeT together and convincing them to fight for Kashmir and against India.

There were several reasons why the jehad in Kashmir was of paramount importance to Zaki. Firstly, the ratio of deployment of forces in Kashmir vis-à-vis the general population was one of the highest. So it became a legitimate struggle, to fight the occupation forces in Kashmir. Plus, there is no denying that Lashkar was closer to the Kashmir situation and population than it was to Afghanistan, which is why it could continue the jehad better in Kashmir than in Afghanistan. Over the years, the LeT had become known as an outfit struggling for the liberation of Kashmir, and this would not be easy to replicate in Afghanistan.

Also, at the time, I knew that the ISI was under tremendous pressure to stop any integration of Kashmir-based jehadi organizations with Taliban-backed outfits. It was always in the interest of the ISI to keep these two sets apart. So Zaki was only reiterating the ISI's official line.

However, the aggression and commitment to jehad shown by the several splinter groups in Afghanistan influenced many committed fighters to leave Kashmir-centric outfits and join the Taliban. This, in a way, compelled the LeT to think up a spectacular terrorist strike in India, and in the ISI it found a willing partner. The strike would essentially serve three purposes: to control further splits in Kashmir-based outfits, give them a sense of achievement, and shift and minimize the theatre of operations from the domestic soil of Pakistan to India.

All of this simply accelerated the Mumbai attack project. Where, initially, it was only a limited plan to attack the Taj with a couple of men, it grew into a grand plan to strike Mumbai at multiple locations with multiple attackers. That was where I had come in, and why my role was so crucial to the ISI and the LeT. And they agreed that I had fulfilled this role with aplomb.

After September 2008, my part in the Mumbai attack was over, and the mission was fully handed over to Lashkar. It was now their turn to show what they were capable of.

SIXTEEN

My friendship with David had grown stronger than before, and I felt as if no two human beings could ever be closer. Our association was the most special thing in my life, and even though David was away for several weeks at a time, we kept in touch with each other by phone, SMS or email. With a dysfunctional family like mine and an absentee father like Mr Mahesh Bhatt, David's presence was the best thing that had happened to me.

Ironically, Vilas had become more of an appendage. My relationship with David was warmer, and more intense than his with Vilas. I couldn't figure out why this was so; maybe there was a language barrier between them, because all said and done, Vilas's English was not exactly the best.

I even wondered whether David actually understood the expletives that Vilas often used in front of him, some of which were even aimed at him—words like madarchod, behenchod and chutiya. Of course, I know now that not only did David understand every expletive as well as any conversations between us in Hindi, he probably knew far more abusive words than we did and could have put both our Hindi and broken Urdu to shame.

Whether David had decided that Vilas was too foul-mouthed a person to be in close touch with, I shall never know. I never used such abusive language, either aimed at or in front of David. Of course, I am no novice and can match the average street thug word for word as far as uttering gaalis is concerned. I actually think an expletive or two helps you express yourself more accurately. But I refrained from using such language with David because I loved and respected him. I told myself that even though David was an American and probably did not understand the words of abuse, I would never use such language with him. Vilas, unfortunately, had no such reservations. And I have to hand it to David—he always kept such a straight, innocent face that I never managed to figure out that he was following the entire conversation.

Those were good days, when David was in Mumbai, and we all hung out together. We would watch movies, eat out, or simply wander around together. We liked spending time with each other.

One day, we were talking about women in general—who would make a good wife and who a better lover and so on—when David told me that I should get myself a Moroccan wife. I was most surprised and asked him why. David laughed and told me that he had a lot of experience when it came to women, and Moroccan women were especially hot and sensuous. 'Rahul,' he said, 'you will never find a woman like a Moroccan woman.'

There was one thought I never could shake off: that David could not be an immigration agent. Or even if he was, it was just a cover. There were too many things the man knew that made me certain that he was part of some intelligence agency.

On 20 September 2008, we were in my Maruti SX4 on our way to watch *Hannibal Rising*. We planned to have dinner together after the movie. As we were crossing Kemps Corner, we heard on the car radio that an explosive-laden truck had detonated just outside the Marriott Hotel in Islamabad, killing at least fifty-four people and injuring over two hundred and fifty. The massive explosion had left a sixty-foot wide and twenty-foot deep crater outside the hotel.

We had been laughing and chatting till then but when we heard about the attack, all of us, including David, fell silent. The enormity of it was disturbing and no one spoke for a long while. David looked grim and thoughtful. After a while, he broke his silence and said, 'You know, Rahul, this kind of thing may soon happen in Mumbai too. So you guys should watch out and keep safe.'

At any other time, I would have laughed, assuming that David was joking, but this time he seemed to be serious. I found the sudden warning rather out of character for David; I had never heard him make such statements before. But because I always thought that David wasn't just an ordinary American immigration lawyer, I didn't question him. Maybe he had some sort of inside information or intelligence. In fact, he had once told me that he had been with the United States Army Rangers. Were they the ones who had given David some inside dope about an attack in Mumbai? After all, he seemed to have inside information about a million things. For instance, he had once told me how terrorists were being trained by the SSG, Pakistan's Special Security Group, and many things about them that I had never heard before.

I kept quiet, wondering if Mumbai was indeed a sitting duck for terrorist organizations. If the earlier blasts at the Gateway of India and on the local trains were anything to go by, David might well be right. We never seemed to learn from our mistakes.

A few days later, David left Mumbai again, ostensibly to go to the US. But we maintained contact. He used to call me at 10.30 or 11 p.m., when I was ready to retire for the day; it was the perfect time to talk to him. Perhaps he knew that, or perhaps it was just convenient for him to call me at that time, but I soon grew used to his calls at night.

He once told me that all these calls he made were from a satellite phone. It surprised me no end, and I asked him, 'Agent Headley! How the fuck did you get hold of a satellite phone?' He laughed, but he never answered my question.

David's concern for me was touching. For instance, when the swine flu epidemic hit India in May 2009 and the number of deaths kept rising, David called me to find out how we were. He said he found the sight of people roaming around with masks on their faces alarming, and enquired if Vilas and I were safe and if our families were all right. I told him that everything was cool. When I asked about his next trip to Mumbai, he only said he hoped to come soon.

I vividly remember one particular phone call from David. It was on 10 November 2008, at 10.30 p.m., when I was about to go to bed. My phone rang, and when I picked it up, I saw the numbers 00000, which told me that it was a long-distance call from a satellite phone. For some strange reason, I felt uneasy as I answered the call, but it was only David, and I breathed easy. Once I started speaking to him, the fleeting apprehension I had experienced before picking up the phone dissipated.

However, the feeling returned soon enough. After we had exchanged news about each other and made small talk for a couple of minutes, David said, 'Rahul, don't venture out towards south Mumbai for the next few days.'

I was puzzled and didn't know how to respond. He asked me if I'd heard him, and I said yes, but when I asked him why, David refused to elaborate, only repeating what he had said. 'Just avoid going to south Mumbai for some time. I thought I should tell you this.'

I was sure that David was not joking, so I said okay, and told him that I would heed his advice. I read in his serious, friendly tone a kind of paternal concern for me, as David had become like a father figure by then. So I did not question him, and agreed to do as he said.

It so happened that there was never any reason for me to go to south Mumbai in the next few days as my work, my gym, everything was concentrated in the western suburbs.

And then it happened. Mumbai was attacked on 26 November 2008 and my life changed.

Like everyone else that night, I watched the horror unfold on the various news channels on TV. Ten commandos were ripping my city apart, there were explosions at the Trident, there had been firing at CST and at Metro, the Taj was up in flames; Mumbai was reeling under an unprecedented, ruthless terror attack. Despite the combined might of the National Security Guard, the elite Marcos, short for Marine Commandos, the navy, army and the Mumbai Police, we took nearly sixty hours to neutralize those ten boys from Pakistan, who later turned out to be mere rookies. They left 166 people dead and several hundred injured. But more damagingly, they left a city and a nation forever scarred.

I remember staying frozen in my seat, numbly watching the carnage unfold. I still cannot believe what happened, and how Mumbai was set aflame and very nearly destroyed by just a few boys from Pakistan. Since then, I have often wondered what would have happened had there been not just ten people but a force of 100. Would the NSG commandos and the army and all our security agencies have been able to stop them even in 600 hours?

As we discovered later, two of the terrorists, Ajmal Aamir Kasab and Abu Ismail, were neutralized right at the beginning. They had drawn their AK-47 rifles and fired indiscriminately at the crowd at CST, wreaking havoc within seconds; fifty-eight people were killed at the railway terminus and over a 100 wounded in the hour-long assault. Two others from the team of ten were at Nariman House, taking Rabbi Gavriel Holtzberg and his family hostage. These two received real-time instructions from their handlers in Pakistan, and were told to kill all the Jewish hostages, as 'the lives of Jews were worth fifty times those of non-Jews'. They killed the rabbi and his wife, who was six months pregnant, and four other hostages, before they were taken out by the NSG. At the Taj were four of the terrorists, two who had gone there directly and two who had first shot and killed ten people at Leopold Cafe before proceeding to the Taj. The other two were at the Trident.

The attacks began close to 9.30 p.m. on a Wednesday night, and ended on Saturday morning at 8 a.m., when the last terrorists were neutralized at the Taj. These four attackers, who were holed up at the Taj, gave the security agencies the toughest time and ended up killing some of the best commandos of the NSG. Everything inside the Taj was damaged, from famous artworks to antique artefacts; the Sea Lounge, where David, Vilas and I had had lunch once, suffered the most damage.

Sadly, even as the terrorists were getting real-time instructions from Pakistan and executing them, our own people, who knew the layout and topography of the city as well as of the individual buildings, could not finish them off sooner. What a shame!

It was not until much later, after all but one terrorist had been killed and Mumbai was struggling to come back to some semblance of normalcy, that I remembered the call that David had made to me a couple of weeks earlier. I had no way of contacting him directly, since it was always he who called me, but one thought kept returning to me constantly—how could David have known about the attack, going to the extent of warning me to stay away from south Mumbai? How could he have known in September, when we heard about the bombing at the Islamabad Marriott, that a similar attack could rock Mumbai, while our security agencies knew nothing about it?

These and many other confusing thoughts kept plaguing my mind. I waited for David to call, so I could ask him how he could have known what would happen, but the call never came.

Then, finally, sometime in the second week of December, my phone rang and I picked it up to see the familiar set of zeros. It was David. It was a huge relief to see the number after all the time I had spent waiting. I pounced on the phone and said, 'Hello, David, how are you doing?'

Uncharacteristically, he did not answer my question. Instead, the first thing he said was, 'Are you and Vilas safe?'

'Yeah, we're fine,' I told him.

'Are your families all right?'

'Don't worry, David, we're all okay, and our families are safe. We're fine,' I said, as reassuringly as I could.

I think I heard a sigh of relief on the other end of the phone. He then asked me what the situation was like in Mumbai. I told him that it was pretty chaotic, and that eight black-suited agents of the US Federal Bureau of Investigation were here too.

'Did you see what they said about the Sea Lounge at the Taj? It's the most damaged!' David said.

I had just been thinking that too.

Then David said he knew about the whole thing. I didn't know what to say, and when I asked him what he meant, he refused to elaborate. I knew it was pointless trying to prise answers out of him, and that it would be better for both of us if I waited until we met. So I asked him when he would come to Mumbai next, and he promised me that he would come and speak with me directly. We said our goodbyes and hung up, but I never met him again.

That call left me with mixed feelings. I couldn't help but wonder about this man who was so concerned about us and our safety. It was clear to me that he was more than he appeared, his last couple of calls had proved as much. My nickname for him, Agent Headley, fit David to the T. But if he was all that and more, why was he so anxious to know if we were all safe? What did we mean to him, to this American who lived so many thousands of miles away? And there was that one thought at the back of my mind which I couldn't blank out, however much I tried. If David was so well informed, if he had known months in advance about what would happen to Mumbai, why had our own security and intelligence agencies not known about it? More specifically, why had he or his bosses not told Indian agencies about the attack?

SEVENTEEN

'Well, Mr Headley, we know what happened on 26 November. What did you do next?' Behera asked.

The top cops from the NIA were still smarting from Headley's barbs about India's security setup, the utter lack of security along the Mumbai coastline, and the ease with which the Pakistani terrorists had managed to exploit the chinks.

They shifted uneasily in their seats and tried to shrug off Headley's censure, at the same time bracing themselves for any more disclosures on the lax vigilance.

'You need to know a few things before I tell you what I did next,' Headley said.

Behera nodded.

I hadn't done much for nearly three months. On my handlers' instructions, I had gone to Mumbai one last time in September 2008, to wrap up my surveillance there. Then I returned to Pakistan, again via Dubai, and passed on my observations to my LeT masters.

After that, I sat around in Lahore, waiting for instructions on further assignments. Time passed excruciatingly slowly, and I was getting restless. It was impossible not to do anything, not be a part of anything! There was no word about my extensive recces in

Mumbai either, and I was getting worried. Whenever I asked Sajid Mir or Major Iqbal what was happening on the Mumbai front, they would ask me to be patient, and assure me that I would soon find out.

Initially, I thought there were some internal problems between the ISI and the LeT. It had been brewing for some time, with major differences cropping up between Abdur Rehman Pasha and the LeT's Zaki-ur Rehman Lakhvi. Zaki felt that he was being upstaged by the ISI, and that the ISI was using him. Once, Abdur Rehman Pasha, Abu Dujana, Major Haroon and I were at my house discussing a plan to assassinate President Musharraf. Later, when Abu Dujana told Zaki about this discussion, he flew into a rage and warned us against such talk. In fact, Zaki and Major Haroon too had a falling out later, and Major Haroon even distributed pamphlets against Zaki. There was also a strong rumour that the ISI would have Zaki removed as the military chief of LeT. However, it did not happen.

Anyway, after sitting around doing nothing for a long time, in the first week of November, I decided to go to my masters and ask them what my next course of action should be.

I contacted Abdur Rehman Pasha and secured an appointment with him. On the designated day, I met him in Karachi, and after paying my respects, I expressed my desire for further assignments. Pasha had already heard of my exploits in Mumbai and had a plan of action ready for me.

The mission this time was the same: surveillance. The target: Copenhagen, Denmark. Specifically, the Aarhus offices of the Danish newspaper *Morgenavisen Jyllands-Posten*.

On 30 September 2005, the *Jyllands-Posten* newspaper had published an article with cartoons of Prophet Muhammad. The entire Islamic world rose up in protest, saying that the Danes were deliberately insulting the Prophet.

Pasha asked me to go to Copenhagen and conduct a detailed

recce of the office, just as I had done in Mumbai, in preparation for an attack on the newspaper. The infidels would pay, he told me, for ridiculing Prophet Muhammad.

I was active again. But I had not been told who would be conducting the operation. I knew that the chances of Lashkar doing it were slim, as the LeT more or less confines itself to the Indian subcontinent. It isn't really active anywhere else. But if not the LeT, who could it be?

I asked Pasha. He told me that if Lashkar did not go through with the attack, someone else would, but he refused to elaborate. He asked me to be patient. 'Allah will provide all the help in this matter,' he said.

However, I had not been a part of the LeT and undergone intensive training for nothing. I had a faint inkling of who might help us in the attack on the Danish newspaper.

In some of my earlier conversations with Pasha, he had mentioned that he was in touch with the famed Ilyas Kashmiri, one of the most important and highly placed men in the hierarchy of the Al Qaeda. He was known as Doctor to everyone. Unlike the LeT, Al Qaeda is a worldwide outfit with access to every corner of the globe. When Pasha remained secretive, my sixth sense told me that Ilyas Kashmiri could be the person. Kashmiri was pretty much the second-in-command at the Al Qaeda after Ayman al-Zawahiri, the outfit's spokesperson—if Zawahiri was the right hand, Kashmiri was the left hand of Osama bin Laden, whom we jehadis always referred to as Amir Osama.

But before anyone would agree to help us, someone would have to show them that some work had already been done, and that surveillance work was already being carried out. That someone was me. I met Sajid, who was in those days coordinating the attack on Mumbai, at a McDonald's outlet in Karachi. He gave me a drive containing some information on Denmark, which was m open-source research conducted on the country. It had information about Denmark and photographs of Flemming Rose and Kurt Westergaard, the cultural editor and the cartoonist, respectively, of *Jyllands-Posten*. Sajid also gave me 3,000 euro for the Denmark reconnaissance.

Armed with information and money, I went to Copenhagen in mid-November and, as instructed, visited the Denmark offices of the newspaper. I couldn't just walk into the office, so I had prepared an airtight excuse for my visit. I explained that First World Immigration was to open a branch in Copenhagen, and as a first step towards making ourselves more visible in the market, we wanted to place an advertisement in the newspaper.

This naturally got the attention of the advertising section, and we sat and discussed the matter in detail until I had convinced them that I was indeed going to open a branch office in Copenhagen, and that I would definitely pay for the advertisement.

After walking out of the office, I went around the building to check the general layout and the security arrangements in place. It was a huge five-storey structure, with several entry and exit points at every level. Once outside the complex, I scouted around and took extensive videos and pictures of not just the newspaper office but also the surrounding areas.

It was with some dismay that I realized that the office was very differently structured and located, and the entire city was very differently planned than Mumbai was. Mumbai lends itself to mayhem and chaos—it is also a city with several entry options, while Copenhagen was a better organized and far more secure city.

When I came back to Lahore and reported to Pasha, I noted with surprise that he wasn't as disappointed as I was. At least as far as I could tell, he seemed to be pleased with the video surveillance that I had conducted and with the debriefing that I had given him. I realized that he probably had expected this and yet had something planned, which is why he didn't share my dejection. It left me feeling very hopeful.

On 26 November, I was sitting and watching television at home, in a flat in Lahore, when there was an eruption of news on all the channels—Mumbai had been attacked by ten men who had seized the Taj and Trident hotels and killed many people and taken many others hostage.

I knew at once that my surveillance had finally borne fruit. Those ten men were doing what they were only because I had got them all the information. I had never met any of them when I was in Pakistan talking to my handlers, but I had heard of them being trained for a mission of utmost importance. They had undergone training for around six months, which is nowhere close to what is needed for a mission of this magnitude. This meant that the ten Pakistani attackers were actually not much better than rookies.

I watched in amazement as the Indian security agencies, which were so arrogant about their so-called elite security forces like Marcos and the NSG, made little headway against the ten poorly trained rookies. Sajid Mir had shown me photographs of these boys sometime ago, and any doubt that I might have had at the time about how effective they would be against Indian security dissipated completely as I watched them tear Mumbai apart.

I felt a surge of pride at our boys and at being the one who had made their mission possible. For a fleeting moment, I remembered the ten wristbands I had bought for them from the Siddhivinayak temple in Dadar, and knew that they were wearing them. It made me proud to see our boys put up a spirited fight against all those heavily armed and well-trained commandos. Surprisingly, the NSG took several hours to reach the Taj, and by that time our boys had already taken control of the hotel, causing maximum damage.

I said a silent prayer for those ten brave men, knowing that they would not make it out of Mumbai alive. But they had done well and would get their due in heaven.

As I continued to watch the progress of the mission on TV channels, I started getting calls from my LeT masters and friends— Lakhvi, Hafiz Saeed, Sajid Mir and some others; the stream of calls put me on cloud nine. My wife Shazia too called me and congratulated me on my successful reconnaissance mission, which had made this attack possible. Of course, she used coded language, but I still understood what she was saying and felt very happy. All my callers told me that it was because of me that they had managed to successfully attack Mumbai. I was also told that I had found my way to heaven through this.

I was itching to do more such work and to get *ajr*, reward for my dead father, who had died in 2007. The success of the Mumbai attacks invigorated me and I decided that I would ensure that the Copenhagen attack became a success as well.

Pasha and I had kept in touch via email all this while. I had also communicated with him over the surveillance in Denmark. I met him again in December 2008, and a couple of times after that. During subsequent discussions, I asked him when we would be able to mount an attack on the *Jyllands-Posten* office. My friend Tahawwur Rana was present at this meeting when I told Pasha that I was fully ready to go ahead with the mission. Rana had also been present when I had returned from my first trip to Copenhagen, dismayed and frustrated, and he was visibly surprised to see the change that had been wrought in me since that time.

Early in January 2009, I consulted Rana on how to go about setting up a branch of First World Immigration in Copenhagen. I asked him if I would need any documents and what I would need to tell any officials who might question me, so as to not arouse any suspicion. Rana told me that the most important thing was to be utterly confident of myself—that was half the battle won. He also gave me a lot of details about the nitty-gritty of his business and told me that it was important that I portray the First World

Immigration business as a very successful one. This, he told me, would automatically allay any fears.

Rana also got some business cards designed for me. These mentioned that I was his partner in the immigration business. The designation on the cards was a mouthful—I was apparently an Immigration Consultant from the Immigration Law Centre for First World Immigration. I was impressed at the ease with which I could take on a new identity, and again felt a surge of excitement. Yes, the Copenhagen operation would be a success.

In January 2009, I made my second trip to Copenhagen. I landed up at the office of the *Jyllands-Posten* newspaper on 20 January, with the same intention as on the last occasion—to place another advertisement in the newspaper. I also made sure to give out several of my business cards to people in the office, and they appeared very happy with the regular business that I seemed to be promising them once my office was set up in the city.

When I visited the office again on 23 January, I started filming in earnest. I used my camera to record the layout of the entire area in detail. I was trying to look at it in the light of all that had happened in Mumbai. I was trying to work out if a similar sort of attack could be carried out in Copenhagen.

But the more I inspected the office and the area, the more keenly I felt that my earlier misgivings had been correct. It would not be possible to replicate the brazenness of the Mumbai attack here. Copenhagen was structured very differently, the security setup was far more professional than the one in India, and to add to it all, the *Jyllands-Posten* office was centrally located in the city and consequently had a very good security arrangement. It would be impossible for even a trained team of jehadis to take this office by surprise.

Just as I had done before in Mumbai, when I reported every detail to Sajid Mir and Major Iqbal, I reported back on Copenhagen to Pasha in Pakistan through email. When I went back to Pakistan, I told Pasha that I believed our primary and only targets should be the newspaper's editor and the cartoonist who had drawn the insulting cartoons of Prophet Muhammad. But Pasha disagreed. He said that everyone in that office needed to die. In fact, he said, all Danes deserved to be killed.

Pasha showed me a video that had been produced by the media wing of the Al Qaeda in August 2008. It claimed responsibility for an attack on the Danish embassy in Islamabad on 2 June 2008. It called for further attacks to avenge the publication of the caricatures of Prophet Muhammad, and pronounced, just as Pasha had done, that all Danes should be killed.

But we were far from the actual operation. After all, we had not even found anyone to sponsor the attack. When I asked Pasha what we would do, he smiled at me and said that all was well, and that there was someone who was more than willing to help us.

In February 2009, Pasha took me to Waziristan in the FATA (Federally Administered Tribal Areas) region to meet Ilyas Kashmiri, alias Doctor.

From the moment that I saw him, I was struck by Kashmiri's appearance. He had a thick beard and wore dark sunglasses, which gave him a sinister look. He spoke with quiet authority, and I could tell that this man knew what he was doing. After all, he was high up in the hierarchy of the Al Qaeda!

He had heard about my contribution to the siege of Mumbai and congratulated me for its success, acknowledging that it had been my reconnaissance mission that had made it possible. We then showed him the videos that I had made of the Danish newspaper office and its surroundings. He seemed pleased with the reconnaissance, and I fancied that he was also satisfied at my abilities and that I was the one who had been selected to carry out this task.

Throughout the meeting, I remained thoroughly in awe of Ilyas

Kashmiri. Also, for the first time, I realized that I was slowly climbing up the hierarchy. After dealing with the Lashkar, I had dealt with Pasha, one of the most highly placed men in Pakistan, and now, here I was hobnobbing with one of the top commanders of the Al Qaeda!

It was finally decided in March 2009 that the Lashkar would not go ahead with the attack on the Danish newspaper because they were under intense pressure from India in the aftermath of 26/11. It was now up to the Al Qaeda—only they and I could carry out the attack in Denmark.

In May 2009, Pasha and I met Kashmiri again. During this period, Pasha and I had gone over all the surveillance videos again and again, planning all kinds of invasions and attacks. When we met Kashmiri this time, he put me on to several of his European contacts. These people, he said, would give me all the money, weapons and manpower that I might need for the attack on the newspaper. I was left speechless. This was fabulous! Unlike the LeT, whose contacts and logistics were limited to Pakistan, Afghanistan and Kashmir, the Al Qaeda had international contacts and reach, and was clearly far more powerful than the LeT. Its operatives were deeply entrenched in European cities and were flush with money. They were also sympathetic to our cause and were willing to place me anywhere and help me in every possible way. However secure Copenhagen was, however foolproof its security, nothing can stand up to a brutal enough onslaught, and I had just been given the means for that.

I realized that Kashmiri had been very impressed by the Mumbai attacks and my role in them. He felt I could be given the authority to go ahead and plan the attack in Copenhagen in exactly the way that I wanted to.

I would not let him down, I promised myself. I would be successful, and earn laurels in such a way that I would be introduced, finally, to Amir Osama.

EIGHTEEN

'So, you met Ilyas Kashmiri at least twice to discuss your Copenhagen operation?' Behera asked.

Headley nodded. 'More than once.'

There was a bit of confusion in my life at this time.

Despite the support of one of the top commanders of the Al Qaeda, who wished me to plan an attack on the *Jyllands-Posten* newspaper office, everyone else seemed to want me to carry out even more surveillance missions in India for future attacks across the country.

So, on the one hand, I had been given instructions to visit India and focus on Jewish targets and synagogues. At the same time, I was also asked to ferret out more information on the Mickey Mouse Project (MMP), also known as the Copenhagen project. Each of these two powerful factions wanted me to work for them— the LeT, which had trained me, and the Al Qaeda, with whose support I could really make a mark in the world.

In such a situation, I was not very clear about what to do. But I made a decision soon—I would work as much as I could for the LeT.

In one of the regular email correspondences with my Lashkar

friends, I was told to move to 'Rahul City'. I checked with them whether they were considering 'investment plans' or 'business plans' there. I was told that it would be more for real estate than business, meaning that more attacks were being planned and I had to scour for more targets.

Although I was gearing up for MMP after having already made two trips to Copenhagen, I decided to go to India again soon after I got these instructions.

I reached Mumbai in March 2009. I stayed at the same hotel in Churchgate, Hotel Outram. Keeping that as my base, I moved around the city. I had been instructed by my masters in Pakistan to record videos of every place in Mumbai that I thought could be a potential target, including synagogues, and also to visit Goa.

So I spent a few days locating possible attack sites and visiting synagogues across the city, starting from Byculla in central Mumbai and moving out to other places. Once I completed my work there, I decided to visit Goa.

When I landed in Goa, I saw that the entire place was teeming with foreigners. It would be a brilliant target, especially since we wanted to grab international eyeballs. But after the Mumbai attacks in November 2008, I had to be careful not to be recognized, even by accident. One never knows how far back any trail goes, and if the Indians tried hard enough, which they certainly were after 26/11, they might stumble onto me and what I was doing. In Goa too, I made sure not to stay in any one place for too long, fearing that I would be traced and found out as the man who had conducted all the reconnaissance and single-handedly helped the ten terrorists attack Mumbai. If I moved around enough, I knew that nobody would be able to trace me. During my two-day stay in Goa, I figured out all the joints that are frequented by foreigners and tourists.

During that trip to India, the final trip that I made to that country, I identified targets in Mumbai and Goa. This time, I made no contact with my friends in Mumbai, Vilas and Rahul. I couldn't risk it. I put all the information and details, including the videos that I had made of the targets, in a report to give to my friends in Pakistan.

I was not contacted immediately after I reached Lahore. During the few days that I had to myself, I kept preparing the plan for the attack, all the while telling myself that I would soon be able to go back to the much bigger international target of the Danish newspaper office in Copenhagen.

In July 2009, I set out on another trip to Copenhagen. I was looking at it as a final surveillance trip to tie up any loose ends. The videos I would make during this visit would help us fine-tune the plan and decide how the attack on the city and the Danish newspaper could be carried out. Of course, this meant that the Rahul City project would be kept on hold for a later date, but I wasn't complaining. Far from it.

Just like on my earlier visit to Mumbai, I made sure that I wasn't in touch with anyone I had met in Copenhagen the previous time I was there. I did not meet any of the people from the newspaper, and made sure that I was not recognized as I wrapped up my surveillance of the office.

Then, one day, on 13 September 2009, all my plans for the future came crashing down. I got a call from Pasha, who told me that MMP might have to be put on hold. I was surprised, because even though I had been sent to India and told to focus on Indian targets, everyone had seemed very keen on the Copenhagen operation. I was filled with a dark sense of foreboding, and I asked Pasha why MMP was being postponed.

'Doctor has got married, Daood,' he told me.

I was shattered. Ilyas Kashmiri alias Doctor had been killed! Pasha was speaking in the code that we used to escape detection by security and intelligence agencies: that somebody had got married meant that he had died and gone to heaven. I later found out that Kashmiri had apparently been killed by US bombs.

But I was determined to go on fighting for the cause of jehad. I told Pasha that I was ready to go ahead with MMP. 'If this *amal* (good deed) is *maqbool* (acceptable) and I get *ajr* (religious reward) for it, I want my father to get that *ajr*,' I told him.

But Pasha replied, 'There is nothing we can do, Daood, at least not for the moment.' He then told me to 'collect my unemployment from the company', meaning I would have to temporarily set aside the mission. After Doctor's 'marriage', I was in a fix and could see no way of going forward, as I didn't even know if his contacts in Europe would agree to fund and help me.

Maybe Pasha sensed that I had taken Doctor's death hard. He tried to cheer me up by saying that it was actually a small loss, and that perhaps some other doctor would 'take over the treatment'. However, I replied, 'No. Doctor's marriage is a major loss.'

After this, I spent several days contemplating what would happen. No one contacted me in those days, and I was again left to wonder what to do and whether we would continue to carry out the Rahul City project, or would have to think of some other project and contact other sponsors.

But Allah was kind. On 21 September 2009, when I had almost despaired of finding any other mission or even sponsors, I got a call from Pasha. The moment I heard his excited voice, I knew he had good news for me.

'There are many reports coming in, Daood. By the grace of God, it seems that Doctor is well!' Pasha said.

It was the best news I had received in a very long time and I could scarcely believe my ears. 'Are you sure?' I asked, elated.

Pasha said, 'Yes, he is well, he's good. Inshallah, he will come back to the hospital very soon.' So Ilyas Kashmiri was not dead after all, and we could pick up the Copenhagen operation from where we had left off.

Delighted at the confirmation, I told Pasha, 'Buddy, if this is true, I will say 100 rakats . . . 100 rakats!' (A rakat can be considered to be a unit of namaz.)

After this, life took a turn for the better. I spent my days figuring out how we would mount the attack on *Jyllands-Posten*. I was waiting for fresh instructions to visit Copenhagen again and resume the project. And with Doctor being alive and well, the instructions came very soon. Pasha called me to confirm that an attack strategy had been planned, and it had been developed with major assistance from my videos.

It was decided that the attack would be carried out sometime in October that year. I worked on a plan over the next couple of months, so that when I met Doctor and Pasha, I would have a strategy in place, to attack the city and the newspaper office.

I felt a subtle change in me as I geared up for the mission. Perhaps because I was now working with the Al Qaeda, who are far more professional than the LeT in terms of their logistics, their funding and their contacts in Europe and the US, I felt more confident. I told myself that Allah was with me, and that I would make a grand success of this mission. It would create a sensation and bring the entire world to its knees. I knew that this time I would not be a mere scout working for the cause of jehad. My role would be far bigger than it had been in the lead-up to 26/11.

NINETEEN

Life is strange, and often unfathomable.

Except for a brief period, when we shared a wonderful rapport during the film shooting in Spiti, my father had been my enemy number one. As far back as I can remember, in the twenty-five years of my life, he was the villain while I was the wronged hero. Just like in the movies, I was the protagonist and my father the antagonist.

But I say that life is strange because despite this, I got a chance to see Mr Mahesh Bhatt in a different light. The recent crisis in my life, thanks to David Headley, gave me a totally different perspective on my childhood and growing-up years. I had heard the age-old saying that blood is thicker than water, but I didn't believe it for as long as I knew David, my David, the good David, not Daood Gilani, the terrorist. But I guess that's the thing about age-old sayings: there's always a grain of truth in them.

After it became clear that I had been cheated and used by David, I spent a long time in an emotional cesspit, feeling depressed and abandoned. But then, as I reflected on the past, certain things started coming back to me, and I realized that all said and done, Mr Mahesh Bhatt had been my saviour on more than one occasion. In fact, he had come to my rescue several times, when I was in trouble or had been wronged. I had just failed to see this in time.

The first such instance dates back to when I was in Class 10 at Learners' Academy. I had always been a slow learner, which frustrated my teachers no end. Ultimately, they decided to throw me out of the school. They wanted a good overall percentage for the school in the board exams so that they could flaunt it and get more students. Since I had failed a couple of times, and was a little slow on the academic uptake, they didn't want to take a risk with me, in case I didn't perform well and brought down the collective percentage of the school. The result: I was expelled.

There was absolutely no need then for Mr Bhatt to come to the school raging like a bull and confront my teacher and give her a piece of his mind. It was more than ten years ago and I was very young, but his stinging words to the teacher still ring in my ear. Mr Bhatt, or maybe I should say Dad, first yelled at the teacher saying that a gross injustice was being done to me. 'As a teacher, you're supposed to be compassionate and nurturing, but what you're doing will ruin his career!' he shouted.

And then he said something that I shall never forget, and which still gives me a warm feeling. Dad said, 'You know what? You can rusticate Rahul if you want to, but it won't be his loss, it will be yours.'

My father's words and the emotional support he gave me during this time amazed me. I still remember exactly how he looked that day, glaring eyes and face flushed with anger and outrage as he kept gesticulating and shouting at my teacher. That was the first time I saw my father stand up for me—against a school that was being unfair to a young child.

I was both happy and confused; happy because I saw that he had come forward to fight an injustice against me, his son, and confused because I had never seen him support me before and had thought that he would never do so. This episode at least should have remained in my mind, and should have given me pause whenever I thought ill of him. But alas, childhood can be cruelly unwise!

This was not the only time that Mr Mahesh Bhatt bailed me out of a tricky situation. There were some other instances as well, some of them quite major. There was the time when I beat up the actor Ranvir Shorey and almost killed him because he had been mean to Pooja. My blows were so powerful and Ranvir was in such bad shape that he had to be hospitalized for a significant period of time. I was arrested. I was afraid that I would have to spend my entire life in prison because of what I had done, but again Mr Mahesh Bhatt stepped in and showed his paternal side. He spoke to me at length, found out exactly what had happened, and ensured that I was kept out of jail and that the controversy was not blown out of proportion. How many fathers would have gone to such lengths, I wonder.

In retrospect, I believe there were many such instances when he came to my rescue. He may not have been with me in my happier moments, but he was always there when I was in trouble.

And of course, he stood by me in my biggest battle yet—the David Headley case. He showed me that he could take responsibility for me after all, and that he had never really deserted me. I shudder to think what would have happened if I had not been Mahesh Bhatt's son. They would have treated me in the same manner that they did poor Vilas. The cops almost broke him and caused so much emotional trauma that he even contemplated committing suicide. I had to keep him safe and functional, and make sure that he did not pop a pill or put a gun to his head or jump in front of a train in his desperation and terror. Of course, it would probably have been far worse for him had Mahesh Bhatt not been involved in my case, and by extension, his too.

Dad didn't spare any means to try and ensure that Vilas and I weren't mistreated. He took the battle right to the NIA, the IB and the Crime Branch, going to the extent of taking on Home Minister P. Chidambaram and even the Prime Minister's Office. He did it with such aplomb that everyone understood that they would not be able to book either of us as an accomplice of Headley until and unless they had concrete evidence, which of course they never had, as both Vilas and I were innocent.

I was impressed by the scathing letter my father wrote to Chidambaram. He told the minister that it was I who had gone to the police, it wasn't as though as though the security agencies had cracked the code themselves. '. . . my son came out like a true patriot and helped the agencies with their investigation, without which they would not have had most of the information that they have now. Instead of using this opportunity to publicly laud these two young men, which would then, in turn, encourage the rest of civil society to do likewise, they are, through their silence, allowing the media to hint at complicity in these men, and to brick by brick demolish the integrity and reputation that we carry in society today,' my father wrote. 'Is this how India chooses to reward its true patriots, who go to unimaginable lengths to assist its agencies?'

Finally, Dad's parting shot in the letter came straight from the heart. 'In this war against terrorism, I am with you, but are you with me?' he asked Chidambaram.

My father's letter to Prime Minister Manmohan Singh was less scathing, but equally hard-hitting. Speaking about how the investigating agencies conveniently kept quiet about the fact that we had ourselves gone to them with information, Dad wrote, 'Is this how India rewards its civil society when it risks everything to stand up for its honour and security? Sir, when those who are vested with authority and power practise injustice and resort to these kinds of games, they devastate the faith of the common man in those institutions that he should be holding in the highest esteem.'

I was amazed to see the extent of my dad's influence, so much so that Dr Singh, who was en route to an international summit, actually replied within twenty-four hours to my father's letter, assuring him that no injustice would be done to me, and that Vilas and I would not be harassed or victimized by the agencies.

I feel now that it is only because of Dad's spirited fight on my behalf that the government agencies did not try to get to me by force or by fabricating evidence. It seems to me that in some of the recent cases in the news, innocent people have been framed and arrested by the police. For that matter, imagine the situation of the two men, Fahim Ansari and Sabahuddin Ahmed, Ajmal Aamir Kasab's co-accused, who were booked on charges of drawing maps for the Pakistani terrorists. Irrespective of whether they are guilty or not, it is strange that no one thought to question that in an era of Google maps and Google Earth and satellite imagery, why would those two men go to the trouble of drawing maps on paper? Unfortunately, such questions are not asked any more. Similarly, they might easily have booked me in the Headley case because by that time, in this country at least, my name had become intricately linked with his.

In fact, it wasn't just my name that was being connected with David Headley. Such coincidences were observed elsewhere in the world as well. But Rahul was synonymous with India, as was evident from the emails that Headley exchanged with his handlers in Pakistan, where they talked about missions in Rahul City. This 'Rahul City' was the code for India, and the terrorists were discussing missions that they could execute in the future.

Despite all this, and probably because of my father's fight and support for us, the NIA guys only took statements from Vilas and me and left us alone. Without him, they would probably have arrested us for interrogation by now.

My father's victory was complete the day the NIA filed a chargesheet in the David Headley case, without citing me as a witness; it proved that Dad had never really abandoned me. I looked at him in a new light, and thought that perhaps his professional compulsions and domestic problems had led him to not pay enough attention to me during my growing-up years, but during crises, he had always been beside me and had always extended his help.

He was still by my side when I got a threat from the gangster Ravi Pujari, who said that he would bump me off because I was 'terrorist Headley's friend'. Dad took the threat seriously, and immediately called me and spoke to me. He then made a few phone calls to the police, and ensured that the cops provided me with security cover. I was given a gun-toting escort to accompany me round the clock.

It is with a lighter heart that I can now admit and confess that despite all the disagreements and disputes that I have had with my father, he has actually been a rock-solid source of support and strength throughout my life, especially in bad times.

I think I should apologize to him one of these days, and make up with him and try to get him to be a permanent part of my life. Maybe that way, I shall have someone to look up to, in times of crises but also someone to share the joys of my life with.

TWENTY

Behera put down the pen with which he was making notes. He had heard enough to make him sick. This man in front of him, he thought, was a maniac. Thank God they had stopped him in time. Who knows how much more havoc and misery Headley would have caused if he had gone unchecked and undetected.

But Headley was still speaking. There was more to come.

My plan was ready, and all I had to do was to convince Pasha that I too was ready. But when we met, he told me to wait, because I would have to tell the Al Qaeda people myself. They were the ones I had to convince, he told me.

And so it was that I travelled to Waziristan again. It was a matter of great pride and honour for me to meet Ilyas Kashmiri for the second time. I could never thank Allah enough for what he had given me, for how far I had come and how much I had grown. I was actually meeting these top personalities who were really close to Allah and were doing such brilliant work in the field of jehad across the world.

It was Pasha again who took me to meet Kashmiri. By now, my respect for him had grown enormously, it exceeded what I felt for

Sajid Mir and Major Iqbal and others from the LeT with whom I had interacted so far. Pasha had his finger in so many pies. And I was constantly amazed by how well connected he was, and the sheer number of people he tapped to get his work done.

When I met Ilyas Kashmiri to discuss the attack strategy, I realized that, like me, he too had been busy designing a plan. We had to ensure that what we did would rock the world. In fact, we had to do it in a much bigger way than the 26/11 Mumbai attacks. It had to be bigger, more sensational, even more shocking than 9/11. We had to ensure that what we did would be a lesson for everyone, and that nobody would take Islam lightly ever again. Of course, our anger and hatred stemmed from the insulting caricatures of Islamic leaders, but it went far deeper than that. With one stroke, we had to pre-empt similar violations in the future.

To this end, Ilyas Kashmiri too had his orders: make this attack deadly, frightening, and gruesome beyond all imagination. He told us that the chieftains of the Al Qaeda—he emphasized that it was the chieftains, the elders—wanted the attacks to not only produce fear in everyone, but also make it impossible for the common man to step out on the street without fearing for his life. I could not figure out who these elders were, though; was Kashmiri talking about al-Zawahiri or Amir Osama or somebody else? Whoever they were, Kashmiri clearly respected their word and, seeing his acquiescence, so did I.

Kashmiri told us his plan. It was brilliant, as it fed on both psychological fear and actual physical shock. First, we would have to lay siege to the *Jyllands-Posten* office and cut off everyone there from the outside world. That itself would create panic as no one would know what kind of horrors were being perpetrated inside.

Second, take everyone hostage and let the world know that the lives of hundreds of innocents were in our hands. That would create fear, and would get the entire world to pay attention to what we were doing.

Third: create debilitating shock. Kashmiri said that none of the hostages would be allowed to live. Each and every one of them would be beheaded, and the heads thrown, one after the other, out of the window, onto the street below. The security forces outside would pick them up one by one, and the television channels would relay all of this live, across the world. It was a foolproof way of creating shock, outrage and panic, and when the world saw the devastation we had caused, it would realize the power and resources we had at our disposal and what we were capable of.

The best part of the plan, we knew, was that if we managed to behead and throw out onto the street the heads of at least ten people, the entire world would come begging to us on its knees to stop what we were doing; they would be willing to accept any and every condition that we set.

I was awestruck at the audacity of Kashmiri's grand plan. It was sheer genius! Of course, at some point, our actions inside the newspaper office would be met with brute force by the security personnel, yet the man was ready and willing to sacrifice everything he had and more for Islam. This spurred me on, and I said that I too had a humble suggestion to contribute.

It was something I had thought of earlier, without being certain that I could take it through to the end. But hearing Kashmiri's plan and having him listen to me with such rapt attention gave me the courage I needed.

I said that this time I was willing to be a *fidayeen*. I was prepared to die for Islam.

At my words, both Kashmiri and Pasha were taken aback for a few moments, and then I saw that they were looking at me with newfound respect and appreciation. This egged me on.

I told them that I would be a suicide bomber. I said that I would strap bombs around my torso and blow myself up in order to gain martyrdom and cause maximum damage to the enemies of Islam.

We might be able to kill each and every person inside that building, but it wouldn't be enough, I said, not in my eyes at least. Once everyone was dead, why not bring the whole edifice down? Why not reduce to rubble and completely annihilate the place where the name of Islam had been dragged through mud? It would be a symbol of destruction, a warning never to underestimate the power of Islam. And to achieve that, I would gladly take on the mantle of a suicide bomber.

I saw that Kashmiri was looking at me quizzically. I told him that I knew my *shahadat* would be greatly appreciated by jehadis everywhere, and my deed, my faith and my martyrdom would encourage other youth to lay down their lives for Islam. What I was proposing to do would give me glory, yes, but more importantly, it would bring glory to the name of Islam.

Finally, they were all convinced that I was serious. Kashmiri smiled, came forward and patted my back, then hugged me tightly. I saw that he appreciated what I was planning to do. Both he and Pasha kept saying *mubarak*. Yes, I thought to myself, this appreciation would definitely reach the ears of the elders of the Al Qaeda. And someday soon I would be hailed as a hero by all my brothers across the world.

There was one final thing I had to take care of. If I was going to do this, if I was going to give up my life, I needed to make sure that my assets were handled and distributed properly and my family looked after. I had to make my will, and for that, there was only one person I could turn to: Tahawwur Rana.

I wrote to him to say that, going by current planning, I wasn't going to make it out of there alive. I told him what to do in such a situation.

I used codes, not names. I told Rana I wanted to get M2 (Faiza) to Canada as soon as possible. Until then, he was to regularly send her $350 through Abdur Rehman Pasha. There was always a chance that Rana's number might be tracked by intelligence agencies if he spoke to M2 himself, so it was imperative that he only communicate with her through Pasha. And after she got her visa to Canada, I told Rana, he should give her $6,000 and a ticket.

I didn't know how to handle the matter with M1 (Shazia) as clearly though, and I told Rana that he would have to sit down with her and figure out when she should return home. He would have to use his best judgement.

I also wanted my sons to get into Aitchison after their Hifz (memorizing the entire Holy Quran), and asked Rana to see if he could work it out.

Finally, I gave him a list of all my properties and their worth, including my shops in Dubai, plots of land in Pakistan, Gharo, and my father's house. I owned 60 per cent of that house, and I told Rana I wanted my sons to keep it at any cost.

My slate was clean. I had done everything, ironed out all issues and doled out everything I owned.

I was getting ready for shahadat.

TWENTY-ONE

In Greek, the word hypocrite means actor, and Headley was both—an actor par excellence and a hypocrite to the core. The man had played with my emotions and cheated me, but it wasn't just me he had done this to. He had scorned each and every person who had come into his life, whether friend, foe, family or complete stranger.

Headley was a mercenary. He wasn't loyal to anyone, not even to his women. He married four women and cheated on each one. He had his masters in the US—the FBI, the CIA and the DEA—but he double-crossed them as well. He was a Pakistani, but he behaved like an American. And when he took on an American name, he was actually an operative working for the Lashkar. When he came to India, he behaved like an American but was actually a Pakistani. It was as if the man was Ravana personified, with ten heads and ten different faces.

I have not been able to decode Headley to this day. He had too many faces. Perhaps this is the reason why the Americans failed to understand him; neither did the Pakistanis. To the latter, he was just someone who helped see their dastardly designs through till the end.

I had read somewhere that people who turn to terrorism generally come from broken families. They don't get enough parental love and compassion, and ultimately turn to the path of violence, so-called jehad. Of course, this does not mean that everyone who comes from a broken family will become a terrorist, but it does imply that almost every terrorist comes from a broken home, where the father ill-treated them and did not give them the friendship and love that they craved. This is why, in search of some kind of bonding and mentoring, they seek refuge in the company of other men, and hardcore terrorists manipulate their emotions and push them towards violence and crime.

With these kinds of thoughts swirling around in my mind, I tried to find out more about the sort of people terrorists are. I started reading books and referring to old literature about terrorism. And I found that Headley shared quite a few similarities with two other terrorists, both perpetrators of the 9/11 attack—Ramzi Yusuf and Mohammad Atta.

Yusuf and Headley appeared to be very similar: like Headley, Yusuf was a charmer, his parents were of mixed origin, and he too turned out to be a mercenary. He liked to charm his way into people's lives and take whatever he wanted. Like Headley, he was very meticulous, very determined and highly intelligent.

Atta, though, was an angry man, and maybe deep inside, so was Headley. Atta, like Headley, had a deep-rooted angst against his father and had a complicated relationship with both his parents.

This was when it dawned on me that I had issues similar to these two. I too have problems with my father, and my parents are from different religious backgrounds and, in fact, different worlds. I am the product of a mixed marriage. It is quite likely that if Headley had not been arrested when he was, I would have become one of them. Maybe I would have become a Yusuf or an Atta or a David Headley junior. I don't know what fate would have had in store for me if that had happened, but I was saved somehow.

I began tracking Headley and his journey on the Internet, through news articles and the documents related to his trial. I wanted to find out how a man like him, a brilliant actor and a covert operative, was finally arrested. How did a man who was such an expert at deceiving all and sundry, manage to fall into the net of the US agencies?

As I browsed online, I came across a story in the *International Herald Tribune*. It said that the Americans had been able to track Headley using the oldest trick of all: they planted a bug on him.

Clearly, Headley had no idea that at some point, the FBI had become suspicious of him and his movements to and from India, Pakistan and Denmark. They decided to keep tabs on him, and planted a concealed microphone in his car. And by doing so, they stumbled onto his devious plans, what he had done and what he was planning to do.

On a long car ride in September, the two Chicago men, Tahawwur Rana and David Headley, spoke openly about the terror attacks in Mumbai and about their future plans in Copenhagen. It was a month before Headley was arrested, and in that crucial conversation, everything came out. I could not get my hands on the full transcript, but the newspaper reported that Rana had been quoted as saying that if there had been one medal in the world for command, top class, 'Daood, you would've got it.'

It was an insignificant comment, but that's how the FBI realized that Rana was actually complimenting Headley for all his achievements and accomplishments in India and future ones in Denmark.

The entire story in *IHT* was about how the bug was first placed because the FBI needed evidence, any kind of proof, against the perpetrators, something they hadn't been able to get their hands on yet. The microphone they placed in the car recorded a huge chunk of conversation and provided the Americans with exactly what they were looking for. All the missing pieces of the puzzle fell into place. During the conversation, Headley and Rana discussed a meeting they'd had in Dubai. At the meeting, Headley recalled, Rana had been told by Pasha that more attacks were about to be carried out. Everything was in motion and going smoothly, he said, and things had started heating up soon after he had left.

'Where and how did all this start, Daood?' Rana asked Headley.

'In Mumbai, yeah,' Headley replied.

'Yeah?'

'Yeah!'

The FBI had got the evidence it needed. They knew now that Headley's nefarious plans had been launched in Mumbai and that he intended to carry out in Copenhagen a sequel to those attacks. They realized that Headley was fully prepared, and that something big was going to happen very soon.

Soon after this, the Americans apparently decided that they could not wait any longer. For them, Indian blood might be cheap and dispensable, but the white blood of the Europeans was very dear and sacred. They decided that before Headley could orchestrate any more devastation, they had to pre-empt him, they had to bring him in.

So, on 3 October 2009, as he prepared to leave Chicago for Philadelphia, from where he would fly to Pakistan, and from there to Copenhagen to carry out the attacks, Headley was arrested at Chicago's O'Hare airport, even before he could board the flight. A total of thirteen video recordings of surveillance that he had carried out in and around the *Jyllands-Posten* newspaper office in Denmark were found on him—damning evidence indeed.

In fact, he would have been caught much earlier had the authorities, both Indian and American, been a little more alert.

Headley had commented, I found out later from some cops with whom I had developed a rapport, that Indians were chutiyas, especially the babus and diplomats. Apparently Tahawwur Rana had made a huge error in his visa application to the Indian embassy for his first-ever visit to India. David felt that if Indian officials had been just a bit smarter, they would have smelt a rat right at the beginning and his first visit and subsequent mission would have been aborted even before it had started. He also claimed that Indian officials were just not as thorough as they should have been and didn't go through the application as carefully as they should have. If they had done so, they would have noticed the huge discrepancy.

I couldn't help but agree with him. Headley was an American and he held an American passport, and so the mistake was never noticed. A white American man is never questioned. He is never wrong.

Moreover, Headley has himself admitted that he had made three mistakes while he was in India, but being the brilliant actor and chameleon that he is, he managed to extricate himself from each tricky situation. Once, he had made the mistake of speaking in Hindi. He was in a taxi and stuck in traffic and had inadvertently cursed in Hindi. He told his interrogators that the taxi driver was astonished at the white man speaking unaccented Hindi, but he managed to cover it up by immediately putting on a heavy accent and claiming that he had picked up the language locally.

Headley also admitted that once, at Outram Hotel, he had left the door of his room ajar and the owner, Mrs Kripalani, had chanced upon him offering namaz. He got away by telling her that he was doing yoga.

Finally, Headley also made the mistake of bringing his burkha-clad Moroccan wife Faiza Outalha with him to Mumbai. It would have been a very costly mistake had he run into any of his acquaintances with her by his side, because there would have been no way for him to explain her away. However, he managed to escape unscathed.

I looked up Faiza Outalha on the Internet, and saw that an Indian journalist had interviewed her. I read the interview transcript with interest, and it only confirmed what I had found out—that David had betrayed not only me, but many others. Faiza even said in her interview that she felt David wasn't a good Muslim, that he used Islam merely as a cover. She said he used to pray like a robot, unfeeling and uncaring. He also used to treat her badly and had lied to her constantly, a fact that ultimately led her to make enquiries about her husband. What she found out shocked her so much that she immediately went to the FBI, even going to the extent of saying that he knew Osama bin Laden to get their attention. She told them that David had links with the LeT, but instead of helping her, she said that her complaint actually ruffled quite a few feathers. One of the Americans, a blond man at the US embassy, even tried to hit her, because all of them thought she was ratting on her husband who was actually one of their own. Faiza said David was an American soldier, a spy who worked for the DEA. They should have stopped him but they did nothing because he worked for them.

Faiza also believed, 120 per cent as she said, that David had had an affair with a Bollywood actress while he was in Mumbai, a fact that must have distressed her no end.

I felt sorry for the poor woman. She was only trying to do the right thing when she found out what a monster David was. In fact, she unknowingly put herself in grave danger, and even went to Hafiz Saeed to tell him about David's LeT connections. At the time, she had no idea who Saeed was, just that he was a religious man. She also knew Major Iqbal, although she never met Abdur Rehman Pasha. Now, Faiza lives in constant fear of death, knowing that they wouldn't hesitate to kill her.

Faiza also said that the two of them had sat watching the 26/11 attack unfold on TV, and she had been startled to see that he wasn't angry at all. She, on the other hand, was badly shaken, as she had stayed at the Taj herself, and to watch it go up in flames was horrifying. She remembered, too, that David had asked her for forgiveness sometime before the attack, saying that he had done something bad. Despite all the evidence, there is one point on which both Faiza and I agree. Headley was playing the role of a real-life Agent 007, a personality he loved to emulate. He wasn't really a killer, and Faiza too believes that.

Right now, Faiza wants to move on. She knows that David isn't rotting in jail, the Americans are taking good care of him. She wants to leave her past with David behind, find a lawyer and get a divorce. Once the FBI arrested Headley, it wasn't long before they picked up others as well. Two weeks after his arrest, on 18 October, his friend Rana was arrested. The First World Immigration office was raided in Chicago. The authorities also raided a Grundy County meat processing plant that was owned by Rana; the plant was sealed right after.

Headley will be tried, yes, but by now, I have figured out how his mind works. He did exactly what was expected of him. As he had done many times in the past, he implicated his colleagues. He was very quick to speak against his childhood friend Rana and turn approver in the case, thus saving himself from the death penalty and putting Rana in even greater danger. Poor Rana! I don't think he had very much to do with the Mumbai attack, except that he allowed Headley to use the name of his business as a front for his activities.

Headley is now being tried in a US court, and has already made a plea bargain where his indictment under twelve counts will be undertaken by the judge and decided upon. But I'm sure that he will get much more leniency from them than his colleagues or his latest victim, Rana, will. Very soon, I know, he will again be working for the American authorities in some other part of the world.

Mr Chameleon, Mr Actor, Headley the hypocrite, will go scot-free after wriggling his way out of the charges against him.

POSTSCRIPT

It has been nearly four years since the horrific terror attacks on Mumbai. Scarred but far from shattered, Mumbai has moved on, as has India. But we have not forgotten what happened on that fateful day. All through these four years, India has kept insisting that the attack was planned on Pakistani soil, and Pakistan has been equally adamant in denying this. However, the capture of David Coleman Headley opened up a Pandora's box of shocking facts, exposing the treachery of Pakistan's ISI and the LeT to the world. But Headley wasn't just a Pakistani terrorist. Although he sided with the LeT and the Al Qaeda and helped carry on the so-called jehad, he was playing the field for the Americans as well.

In many ways, the Mumbai terror attack was Headley's own *Shawshank Redemption* moment. In this cult Hollywood flick, the protagonist Andy Dufresne goes to jail and eventually escapes by tunnelling through the prison walls, crawling through a sewer, and acquiring his freedom in the dead of night. But this wasn't something he did on the spur of the moment. Andy's plan required him to literally chip away at it for several years. Each night when the prison lights went out, he would remove a tiny bit of rock from his prison cell to get closer and closer to his eventual escape. In the meantime, he slowly won the confidence of the crooked warden to the extent of maintaining the accounts of his ill-gotten money.

Similarly, Headley won the confidence of his American masters to earn his freedom. Headley was serving probation for a conviction in a drug case. But it was terminated abruptly, with three years still to go, in November 2001 and he was sent to Pakistan. The objective was to shift him from anti-drug work to gathering intelligence in Pakistan.

In his documentary *The Perfect Terrorist*, *ProPublica* correspondent Sebastian Rotella quoted US officials as saying that Headley remained an operative for the DEA in some capacity until as late as 2005. Headley has himself testified that he did not stop working for the DEA until September 2002.

Which brings us to the moot point: was he or wasn't he? Was David Headley in cahoots with American Intelligence agencies or did he succumb to the call of his Pakistani roots? David Headley's real identity is a conundrum. India has her own views. Former Home Secretary G.K. Pillai has clearly stated that the possibility of Headley being a double agent is a fairly credible one.

Pillai was in charge of the hectic parlays between the US and Indian governments after Headley was arrested, and is one of several senior Indian officials who is convinced that Headley was actually a double agent. Speaking exclusively in an interview with me, Pillai listed several reasons that led him to conclude that Headley was an American agent.

First, Headley has worked for a period of twelve years for the DEA. It is a known fact that the US never lets go of anyone who has worked for them for so long. During this time, Headley would most certainly have found out a lot about his American handlers and their activities, information which cannot be allowed to fall into outside hands. There is also the investment factor. If the US has put in all that time and money and effort into getting Headley to work for the DEA, they will not let it all go to waste; they are likely to try and use it in some way. Either way, the implication is that he still works for them.

Second, Headley managed to change his name *and* get a passport issued in a new name. Over and above that, his passport has only his mother's name on it, which is very rare. In fact, Pillai believes that Headley is perhaps the only American who doesn't have his father's name—Salim Gilani—on his passport. What is most surprising is how the US authorities allowed the passport to be issued in his changed name without any mention of his father's name on it.

The third reason, Pillai said, that speaks volumes about Headley's ties with the US, apart from his ties with the Islamic terror groups, is that he flitted in and out of Pakistan and India eight or nine times in the last three or four years. The entire world knows how paranoid the US is about its security, especially after 9/11. And it monitors closely those who it is even slightly suspicious about. Heaven help you if you are a Muslim man travelling frequently between Pakistan or India and the US. In such a setting, therefore, it is suspiciously strange that Headley was never questioned or intercepted. His frequent calls to and from Pakistan too were never intercepted, which is something the US always does. But with Headley, the communication channels always remained open and unhindered.

Pillai's next point was about the extradition treaty that India has with the US government. If a criminal involved in crimes in India is apprehended on US soil, India has the full right to ask for the criminal to be deported, and the US has to oblige. When he went on trial, Headley made a plea bargain with the US: he would cooperate fully, and in exchange, he would not be extradited to

India, Pakistan or Denmark. Surprisingly, despite the extradition treaty, the US agreed. 'Why, without consulting the Indian government, did they hastily agree to Headley's plea bargain of no extradition, if they did not have a vested interest?' asks Pillai.

Then there was the question of getting access to Headley after his arrest. Not only did it take a very long time to be given access to him, but also, the NIA was only granted limited access. 'We were clearly told what to ask and what not to broach,' Pillai said. 'If you allow us to interrogate Headley, why would you say that there are certain questions that cannot be asked? It can have only one answer. They knew that if we delved into uncomfortable territory during our interrogation of Headley, the role of the US would definitely come up, which, of course, they didn't want.'

One of the most interesting points, Pillai said, was that the US had already been given several indications of Headley's jehadi leanings by his wife and girlfriend. Most of this input had come in the aftermath of 9/11, when Headley had apparently told his girlfriend that the US deserved what it got. However, at the time, the US admitted to having received so many such inputs that they did not take it seriously.

They should have taken note of Headley and the warnings at least after 26/11. But he travelled unhindered to and from Pakistan and India. This could only mean one thing: that he was moving around with the blessings of the US government.

Pillai also brought up the US intelligence input to Indian agencies. It has been reported that the Americans had informed the Indian intelligence agencies about an impending attack via the sea route sometime in August 2008. However, Indian agencies did not take it as seriously as they should have, treating it only as a routine input. But the US didn't mention the source of the information—that it had come from one of their own inside informants. Had they done so, it would have been treated with far greater importance. But the US ensured that the source was kept a secret, which they would have had no reason to do if Headley hadn't been working for them all along.

Lastly, some US citizens—among them, relatives of those who had been killed at the Taj—have raised a point in a US court: how could the court accept Headley's plea bargain when he had been involved in the killing of Americans abroad? By US law, a plea bargain by a killer of Americans is never accepted. Why was it done this time? The fact that the plea bargain wasn't revoked means that the US definitely stood to gain by protecting Headley.

The former home secretary also raised a very pertinent question: why has the judge not passed a sentence on Headley despite the completion of the trial months ago? He suspects that even if Headley is given the ninety-nine-year imprisonment term, it will be a mere farce. He will be brought out and the US will give him a new identity, perhaps even alter his face with a little plastic surgery, and send him out to work for them elsewhere.

But despite the convincing argument, this theory needed to be vetted. After all, there are those who believe that the statement of a bureaucrat doesn't hold much water once he is out of office. My quest took me to a former agent of the CIA, a man also closely associated with the case. The ex-CIA man agreed to talk to me via email on condition of anonymity and provided fresh insights into Headley's personality. I quote verbatim from his email:

Me: *Was DH a double agent?*

'Depends what you mean by that. He was at least a quadruple agent: DEA, LT, ISI and Al Qaida at the end. The point is that when people seem to work with so many organizations, he is not controlled by anyone of them. He is really working for #1, namely himself. He seems to use other organizations when it fits him. He is definitely NOT a controlled asset of any one of them. He is more of an excitement addict, willing to play ball with anyone that would provide him the means to do so. If you had watched the 14-day interview by the FBI upon his arrest, you realize that he was definitely NOT an American asset. He had used the DEA when it was convenient for him to do so. When he returned to Pakistan in late 2001, he was really his man, leaning toward LeT,' wrote the former US intelligence man.

Headley was apparently plucked out of LeT and put in the big league after his handlers in Pakistan were convinced that he was an asset. The American view is that he was rejected by the FBI Joint Terrorism Task Force and the CIA. The intelligence community in the US is said to have seen through his unstable nature—among other things, he was into steroids to boost his bodybuilding. They thought he was unreliable and a liability who might even claim lives and expose agents. The DEA thought he was manic and exhibited pathological tendencies. The FBI thought he had a violent temper with a history of wife-beating.

Given Headley's identity issues and complex past, the ISI homed in on him because they thought he fit their bill perfectly. Despite his American connection, they touched base with him because he was essentially an Islamic fundamentalist with deep roots and a history in Pakistan. His US passport, fair complexion and western name were added assets that could be used in countries like India. In his interrogation reports, he is reported to have spoken of how the ISI took him under its wing and gave him a complete makeover, including the standard ISI case officer course, counterintelligence, counter surveillance, surveillance, comms, cover, VoIP, mobile security, etc. After 26/11, the LeT came under fire, so Headley switched to the HuJI and set off on his suicidal mission to Denmark, to finish his wasted life in an act that he, in his warped mind, thought would bring meaning to his existence.

But does all this make Headley a double agent, as Pillai believed? Yes and no, says the former CIA agent. 'Headley only worked for DEA, and he was not a controlled asset when in Pakistan. In the post-9/11 environment, there was hysteria in USG security agencies about the nature and size of the threat. It was reasonable that one agency (DEA) allowed him to go back to Pakistan to gather information, no longer on the drug trade but on the security threat to the US. It seems that after his return to Pakistan, it was impossible for the DEA agent in Islamabad to meet and control the asset in Lahore. It may also be the case that Headley was run out of New York, and the Islamabad guy was not really aware of his new tasking. In any case, Headley just let his relationship with DEA lapse and moved on to sign on with Lashkar Toiba. I'm not aware of a formal termination with DEA, it simply lost touch with him,' he explained.

The Guardian's Adrian Levy disagrees with Pillai. He feels that the US government's refusal to allow access to Headley does not mean that he is a double agent. According to Adrian, the US always acts with naked self-interest, cajoling and threatening others around to its point of view, even if it goes against their national interests, and even if it means trading a plea bargain with Headley in Chicago to shut out India, or undermining cops in London who were working on the biggest anti-terror inquiry post 9/11, just to win an election back home.

In August 2006, while British detectives and spies were running a £35-million inquiry into the so-called liquid bombers plot—

British Islamist terrorists with links to Pakistan were being secretly monitored as they experimented with smuggling liquid bombs inside soft-drink bottles onto airliners that would have been blown to pieces—the US ordered the snatching of protagonist Rashid Rauf, a British expatriate living in Pakistan, and that too without telling London.

Certain that news of Rauf's arrest in Pakistan would cause those being monitored in the UK by British security services to take flight, thus skewering one of the most significant police inquiries in years, furious and incredulous detectives were forced to roll up their inquiry in the UK too soon, and before sufficient evidence had been harvested.

But it worked for the US. With a mid-term election coming up in America, George W. Bush could point to Rauf's arrest as a coup in his war on terror. Adrian remembers how in London, the police looked on in dismay and disgust at the ruins of their complex inquiry.

So when Headley, the central witness to the largest act of terror in the Indian subcontinent, was allowed to cook a deal, one that denied India free access and ensured he was never extradited, there weren't many expressions of surprise. 'Business as usual' was the refrain you were most likely to hear in Westminster and New Scotland Yard. 'The US putting itself first as usual.'

Be that as it may, the former US intelligence man firmly debunks the notion that America had an inkling of the Mumbai attack. 'Not true that the USG knew about Mumbai in advance. One just needs to see the questions of the 14-day interview by the FBI after Headley was arrested. This is simply the over-fertile imagination of some commentators who try to link stuff instead of simply relying on facts. Besides at the time, I was part of the intelligence community, monitoring threats worldwide, and there was no advance notice of Mumbai,' he said.

What is absolutely clear is that David Headley or Daood Gilani was nothing more than an 'excitement junkie' who masqueraded as a jehadi. Headley was making a fool of everyone and taking them for a ride. He deceived Americans, leading them to believe he was helping them in maintaining homeland security. He conned Pakistanis into trusting him as a reformed Muslim who wanted to serve Islam. He convinced Rahul Bhatt that he was willing to fill the shoes of an absentee father. But everywhere, he was only playing people along. In the process, he enjoyed life, he had his women and drugs, he travelled, he had access to a lot of money. He was like so many other jehadis who very conveniently circumvent religion when it comes to enjoying the pleasures of life.

Take, for instance, Faisal Shaikh, the kingpin of the Mumbai train bombings of 2007; he had a girlfriend named Manisha, who worked in a bar in the north-eastern Mumbai suburb of Chembur. While working at *The Indian Express*, I managed to interview Manisha, who told me that Faisal regularly visited the bar, though he did not drink; Manisha was paid handsomely for services rendered.

I also checked with the late Shahid Azmi, a lawyer who represented several train bombing accused, on the double standards of jehadis. Azmi, who himself believed in the Salafi brand of Islam, said, 'There are decrees issued by muftis and priests making special exemptions and bending Islamic laws to favour the Mujahideens.' Azmi was later murdered.

Well, what can we say about the mullahs and muftis and priests? They thrive on fatwas to push the community into medieval times. A fatwa was issued on 28 October 2011 by the jehadi forum

Minbar Al-Tawhid Wal-Jihad (the pulpit of monotheism and jehad). Sheikh Abu Humam Al-Athari, a member of its Shari'a council, unequivocally permitted a mujahideen to capture the women of infidels and have sexual intercourse with them, even those who were married, on the grounds that their marriage bonds were dissolved as soon as they were taken captive. These women were regarded as 'maale ganimat' or spoils of war. There are even instances when sodomy was said to be permissible, as the applicant sought to enlarge the cavity in his rectum so that he could carry explosives in it for suicide missions!

One only wishes Muslims would adhere to the Quranic teachings and the peaceful preaching of Prophet Mohammad. The Quran has clearly said: 'If you kill one man unjustly, it is like killing the whole of humanity, and if you save one human life, it is like saving the whole nation (Holy Quran, Maedah: verse 32).'

Headley is a perfect example of the consequence of misinterpreted and distorted teachings of the Quran, given a free hand as he was, and an excuse to kill. But will somebody explain to me this: Where is the license for jehad and indiscriminate, inhuman killings in the name of religion?

Headley has left an indelible scar on the soul of Mumbai. There are many who will never be able to forget or forgive his hand in the betrayal. But many others have tried to move on. Vilas has married, and his wife Sujata and he live happily in the heart of the city, secure in the knowledge that the cops don't suspect him any more. But mention Headley to him and his eyes take on a glazed look.

Rahul Bhatt, the man who pined for a father figure all his life, felt the gravest impact of the betrayal. He occasionally has feelings of loss, hurt and abandonment, but he is looking into the future with his real father, Mahesh Bhatt, and will soon be seen in a movie. His eyes get misty at the mention of Headley; he still misses David's company. But Rahul hopes that someday he will find his place under the spotlight. As Andy Dufresne said in *Shawshank Redemption*, 'Hope is a good thing, maybe the best of things, and no good thing ever dies.'

And Headley? Well, it is only a matter of time. Whatever happens, there is no doubt that he will not end his life in the electric chair. He will be out soon, Agent Headley, working for the Americans again. We can only hope that he, and the other David Coleman Headleys of this world, will not be allowed to wreak any more havoc on mankind.

DAVID HEADLEY'S VISITS TO INDIA: A TIMELINE

FIRST VISIT:
14 September 2006 to 14 December 2006

SECOND VISIT:
21 February 2007 to 15 March 2007. Had married Faiza, medical student in Lahore, in the last week of February 2007, before this visit; went back to Lahore to attend to personal issues.

THIRD VISIT:
20 March 2007 to 17 May 2007: Left Mumbai to spend three days with Shazia and kids in Dubai. Handlers didn't know of this, only Rana did.

FOURTH VISIT:
20 May 2007 to 7 June 2007: Celebrated Vilas's birthday.

FIFTH-SIXTH VISITS:
4 September 2007: Came to Delhi, reconnaissance of NDC. Came to Mumbai same evening. Reconnaissance of Taj (Jazdar), Sena Bhavan, Mathoshree, Pune (he would visit Pune twice in later

years); went to Lahore for Eid for four or five days. Handlers didn't know, Rana did. After returning to Mumbai, he met Rajaram Rege, visited Willingdon golf course.

SEVENTH VISIT:
10 April 2008: BARC reconnaissance. Boat rides the same evening from Taj, Marine Drive.

11 April 2008: Cuffe Parade fishermen's colony.

12 April 2008: Boat ride.

14 April 2008: More conversations with fishermen.

EIGHTH VISIT:
1 July 2008 to 31 July 2008: Taj, Mumbai Police headquarters, bought wristbands at Siddhivinayak, Chabad House; visited Osho's ashram in Pune.

FINAL VISIT BEFORE 26/11:
September 2008: Conversation with Rahul on Marriott Islamabad bombing.

FINAL VISIT AFTER 26/11:
March 2009.

Author's Note: This is the actual timeline of Headley's visits to India. In the main narrative, I have not adhered to the chronology, but instead focused on the nature and significance of his movements during these visits.

SOURCES

This book is the result of extensive collation of information from various sources, including official records, files and documents from investigating agencies of many countries, interviews with several high-profile investigating officials and figures of authority as well as news reports.

One of the most important sources of information was the unabridged statement that David Headley gave to officers of India's National Investigation Agency as they interrogated him for a period of seven days for over thirty hours.

Excerpts from the dossiers that the US FBI Joint Task Force maintained on Tahawwur Rana and David Headley have been used. These were made available by Adrian Levy.

I have also used excerpts from the interview of David Headley's wife Faiza Outalha by Shammy Baweja for Headlines Today.

Some details have been taken from the case files of the trial of David Headley in a Chicago court.

Apart from these, I have accessed news reports that appeared in the *Chicago Tribune, Philadelphia Inquirer, New York Times, Washington Post, The Times of India, The Indian Express, The Hindu,* among others, as well as agencies like the Press Trust of India, Indo-Asian

News Service and Reuters. Some of the major articles that I have used include:

(i) 'FBI knew of activities before Mumbai attack' by Brian Bennett, *Tribune*, Washington Bureau, 18 October 2010.

(ii) 'Local man cited in India attack' by Jeff Coen and Josh Meyer, *Tribune*, 8 December 2009.

(iii) 'US urgently briefs India in effort to head off attacks' by Josh Meyer, *Tribune*, 13 December 2009.

(iv) 'Chicago terror suspects were bugged' by Jeff Coen and Josh Meyer, *Tribune*, 15 December 2009.

(v) 'Business an alleged terror front' by Antonio Olivo, *Tribune*, 3 January 2010.

(vi) 'Trial will probe alleged Chicago ties to Mumbai attack' by Annie Sweeney, *Tribune*, 5 May 2011.

(vii) 'Pak PM's PRO admits he is Headley's half-brother' by Sachin Parashar and Vishwa Mohan, Times News Network, 29 November 2009.

(viii) 'Headley provides more details about Mumbai attacks' by Sebastian Rotella, *Washington Post*, 24 May 2011.

(ix) 'Headley travelled to India nine times on business visa', Express News Service, 9 November 2009.

(x) 'American suspect in Mumbai attack was DEA informant' by Joseph Tanfani, John Shiffman and Kathleen Brady Shea, *Philadelphia Inquirer*, 15 December 2009.

(xi) 'DEA Deployed Mumbai Plotter Despite Warning' by Ginger Thompson, Eric Schmitt and Souad Mekhennet, *The New York Times*, 27 November 2010.

(xii) 'Before '08 Mumbai attacks, US was warned key figure in plot had terror ties' by Sebastian Rotella, *ProPublica*, 16 October 2010.

(xiii) 'In alleged terror plot, a troubling twist' by Sebastian Rotella, *Tribune*, 31 October 2009.

(xiv) 'David Headley and Tahawwur Rana arrested in Chicago', *Global Jihad*, 28 October 2009.

ACKNOWLEDGEMENTS

This book was never planned; it was born out of fortuitous circumstances. On a dull Sunday morning in July last year, I received two calls that set it off: one from Bollywood journalist Subhash Jha and the other from Rahul Bhatt, who later became a friend and co-author of this book. Both wanted me to tell the story of David Headley. Rahul, on his part, was keen that I write about Headley's betrayal.

At the time, I was in the middle of two other books, and was also wary of the transnational nature of the subject, as it would mean a lot of research across countries. And of course, I did not have a publisher for the book. As always, it was Velly Thevar, my wife and teacher of seventeen years, who exhorted me to take the plunge. And as I never say no to her, even if it means jumping off a plane without a parachute, I dived into the project head-on.

My colleague and friend Aditya Prakash Iengar assured me that he would be willing to don many hats for the smooth sailing of the project. A Tambrahm masquerading as a blue-blooded Bong, Aditya started off as my literary agent. He reverted soon enough with the good news and the bad news. He said several publishers were interested, but they wanted the manuscript in a couple of weeks, as Headley's trial was ongoing in a Chicago court.

At the time, I was wrapping up *Dongri to Dubai*, and there were a lot of loose ends to be addressed. I have to admit that but for Adi I would never have been able to wrap up *D2D* so fast and start off on Headley. He also dedicated himself sincerely to 'Rahul and I' and helped me transcribe notes, plot the story, pore over the FBI documents. If I could accomplish this feat and finish the book in record time, it is solely due to him. Thank you so much, Adi.

It was quite a task, interviewing Rahul for hours at a stretch. And for that, I would like to thank Velly, who is a great listener and got the best out of Rahul.

My special thanks are reserved for my publisher, V.K. Karthika, an acquaintance since my *Black Friday* days, who eventually became a very special friend. Karthika showed understanding and patience in giving me a reasonable time frame to finish the project. She was immensely helpful and her support was very reassuring. Thank you, Karthika, you are amazing. I would also like to thank her other colleagues at HarperCollins, especially Shantanu Ray Chaudhuri, Bidisha Srivastava, Shuka Jain and Arijit Ganguly.

Members of the Bhatt family showed immense courage and brutal honesty, which contributed to the story becoming poignant and interesting. Mrs Kiran Bhatt opened her heart and house to me at all hours; Rahul has always maintained that she instilled a strong sense of humanity in him and kept him on the right path in life. Pooja Bhatt didn't mince words and was extremely straightforward. They love Rahul and stood by him during his worst times, but didn't spare his shortcomings. Rahul's girlfriend Deepti Sethi too stayed up sleepless nights with him, helping him with his dyslexia and articulating his thoughts.

Mahesh Bhatt or Bhatt saab is the most forthright man I have met on this planet. I was apprehensive that the story would open up some wounds and that he might not like his dirty linen washed in public, to use an old cliché. But Mr Bhatt told me his side of the story without any fuss. The master storyteller that he is, Bhatt saab gave me his take on Rahul and also on how the controversy provided right-wing elements the fodder to whip up a frenzy against the Bhatt clan. But he took them on, knocking on the doors of no less a person than the prime minister of the country in the process.

Headley and Rahul's trainer friend Vilas Warak may be a man of Hanuman-like quadriceps and Sylvester Stallone-like biceps, but he is tender of heart and a simple man. He was treated shabbily by the investigating agencies because of his humble background. The Headley controversy pushed him to the brink and at one point, he was on the verge of ending his life. I found him very cooperative and affable in the course of my interactions with him for this book.

Among the law enforcers, my gratitude goes to the National Investigation Agency (NIA) chief, Special Inspector General of Police Loknath Behera. Mr Behera's cooperation and helpfulness are beyond description. Despite the deluge of work and his professional compulsions, Mr Behera helped me understand the Headley saga and other peripheral aspects of the story. For putting me on to Mr Behera, I must thank my film-maker friend Kabir Kaushik.

No story of mine is complete without a contribution from Mr Rakesh Maria, the chief of the Maharashtra Anti-Terrorism Squad (ATS). From *Black Friday* to *Headley and I*, the man has been a constant benefactor. I shall never tire of thanking him; I think after Velly, it is him that I owe most.

Former Crime Branch officer of the Mumbai Police and encounter specialist Sachin Waze too helped me with information, as he himself was in the middle of writing a book on Headley. Sachin graciously shared his notes and exclusive photographs, and also postponed the release of his own book. Thank you, Mr Waze.

My journalist friends who chipped in were a class apart. Harinder Shammy Baweja of Headlines Today is one of the top investigative journalists in the country today. She has incredible spunk and resourcefulness and is a very large-hearted person. Journos like Shammy are a rarity. She willingly shared most of her work on Headley, including the preliminary statements and her interviews with Headley's wife, Faiza Outalha. Few journalists are so generous with their colleagues. Shukriya, Shammy.

British journalist Adrian Levy of *The Guardian* was another friend who plied me with heaps of documents and scores of emails full of information, all of which left me with a surfeit of data on Headley. Adrian went beyond the call of duty and provided me with several top-class international contacts as well, who brought in fresh insights on the international ramifications of the Headley incident. Thanks to Adrian's research and investigation, which he shared with me, at one stage it almost seemed like we would have to do a multi-volume edition of the book! I am proud to know you, Adrian, and shall remain indebted to you for adding so much muscle and steel to the book in your inimitable manner.

I would like to extend my gratitude to Adrian's American friend, writer, psychiatrist and former CIA officer, who has long studied terrorism networks. He refused to be named for obvious reasons. These are men who operate in the shadows, anonymous and unsung.

If you find this book informative, it is due to the help of these friends and associates who selflessly contributed to the book. To them goes the credit of the positive attributes of *Headley and I*; the errors and inaccuracies, if any, are solely mine.